BARBARA GYURA

LIGHT OF MY EYES
NAIL

Published by
Hasmark Publishing, judy@hasmarkservices.com

Copyright © 2017 Jennie LynnBarbara Gyura
First Edition, 2017

No part of this book may be reproduced or transmitted in any form or by any means, electronic or mechanical, including photocopying, recording or by any information storage and retrieval system, without written permission from the author, except for the inclusion of brief quotations in a review.

Disclaimer

This book is designed to provide information and motivation to our readers. It is sold with the understanding that the publisher is not engaged to render any type of psychological, legal, or any other kind of professional advice. The content of each article is the sole expression and opinion of its author, and not necessarily that of the publisher. No warranties or guarantees are expressed or implied by the publisher's choice to include any of the content in this volume. Neither the publisher nor the individual author(s) shall be liable for any physical, psychological, emotional, financial, or commercial damages, including, but not limited to, special, incidental, consequential or other damages. Our views and rights are the same: You are responsible for your own choices, actions, and results.

Permission should be addressed in writing to Barbara Gyura: gyurabarbara1971@gmail.com and gyurabarbara@lifechanger.hu

Editor, Sigrid Mcdonald
http://www.bookmagic.ca/

Cover and Book Design, Anne Karklins
annekarklins@gmail.com

ISBN-13: 978-1-988071-43-5

ISBN-10: 1988071437

*I dedicate this book to the
lights of my eyes who mean the world to me: my children:
Csingiz, little Nail, and Rinát.*

TABLE OF CONTENTS

Preface	6
Chapter 1: The Farewell	9
Chapter 2: Nightmare at the Children's Hospital	49
Chapter 3: In Parentheses	70
Chapter 4: Interlude	73
Chapter 5: Hell on Earth	74
Chapter 6: The Tiny White Coffin	128
Chapter 7: The Slow Awakening	147
Epilogue and Afterword	177
Contact Information	197
About the Author	200

PREFACE

This book is about our story. A piece of our life, as it is, in the light of truth. I have no interest in changing it, making it up or taking anything away from it.

We live in a cruel, almost barbarous world, which is perfectly reflected in the series of tragedies of my little son whether he would be with us today if fate had decided otherwise.

If he had recovered, probably I would have never taken my pen in hand to record our adventures in the crazy maze of Hungarian pediatrics from which – in our case – there was no way out. And then it would have been easier to endure the untold pain and humiliation we had to face.

I am a mother. A mother, in the classic sense. I could say that *I am just a mother*. Therefore, I am pretty sure I am biased toward what happened to my son. It would not be too far-fetched to state that I have gone mad a little along the way. It is very difficult to cope with such a loss without losing your mind. Or, at least, I think it is.

Nevertheless, I will try to tell you our story as faithfully as possible.

I am an average educated woman without any medical qualifications. These references are from a layman's point of view, based on my own experience and research.

Since I don't want to libel anyone, I made our story completely anonymous. Sadly, it could have been set in any Hungarian healthcare facility.

Our story is not a specific one in this respect but, on a larger scale, it is a social diagnosis.

Thank God, I know excellent physicians, healers, and great nurses. Therefore, I don't want to overgeneralize.

As I have written in the book, after my son passed away, physicians became my ultimate enemies (or anyone who worked in the healthcare field, for that matter). It took me months to realize that it is actually not them but my self-torturing helplessness that is the focus of my anger.

I hope that publishing the reconstructed version of our tragedy makes the readers create their own resolution and that the characters in our story have a moral compass, and they are capable of feeling remorse. I hope so. Maybe.

Because I ask: Where is the limit? Where are the grounds for human dignity or the respect for a child's soul?

There are so many things that should have been done differently.

What hurts me most is the lack of involvement in the healing procedure, the personal, equal relationship with doctors and the everlasting thought it created: maybe I could have done more. Until this day, I don't know. I can only guess what happened since nobody ever came forward to me with a professional explanation about the course and cause of the disease and sudden death. Although I had been witness to both processes, and saw everything that happened right in front of my eyes, I never received an explanation. Let's say it: even the doctor giving the treatment was not honest with me.

And it hurts very much.

All in all, after asking the opinions of multiple people, supported by facts, I came to the individual conclusion that my barely one-year-old son's tragedy was indirectly caused by an undetected and therefore (for a long time) untreated base-disease (leukemia), and directly, by an insufficiently prepared surgery and unfulfilled conditions of post-treatment together.

But there is more to the truth…

There are many moments with many people, for which I will be eternally grateful for medicine and its practitioners. First, Nailka's birth and that, although he had been diagnosed when he was almost one year old, he'd been with us for twenty months. And I also thank doctors, nurses, and everyone else for the honest and encouraging looks and smiles, twinkling and rolling tears, awkward hand-holdings, and those most telling silences of "mute" lips in moments when every spoken word was just another stab for my wounded soul.

I will always be thankful to our doctors for those last six weeks when they – as a strange gift of fate – allowed us to take Nail home and encompass him with our fanatical devotion, caressing love allowing us to send him from within the embracing wings of family harmony on his journey with the angels. Despite what happened, I will remain grateful to the two children's institutes for allowing us to remain at Nail's side day and night. These two crucial facts changed my life. I had the chance to build such an intense relationship with my child that made the last years seem like years or decades. During these six months, Nail and I had become interwoven to such an extent that every second that passed felt like a whole day. Or maybe months, years? It doesn't matter; we'd already passed the boundaries of time, space, and dimensions.

Today he's far away but keeps coming back to me. Not even death could sever our connection.

I believe that one day, the old, feudal doctor-patient relationships will change and become dignified. Achieving this is our joint task.

Doctors and nurses are only fallible people too, nothing more. They make mistakes, and it hurts me with a burning pain even if I know that there are innumerable people who owe them their lives. But I lost the one who was the most precious to me: the fruit of my womb, my dear little son.

It has been two years that on 6th September 2000 he left.

Since then I have become able to communicate once again, read stories, sing lullabies, rock a cradle, to be a mother. But don't be deceived.

I can take off my mourning clothes, but my heart will forever remain dressed in black. I can laugh at funny moments, but sadness will always lurk at the side of my mouth. I can be a proud mother during the days but visit far away planets at night.

Our life, my life, can never be the way it was – carefree and complete.

Barbara Gyura
Nail Haszjanov's mother

Chapter 1

THE FAREWELL

It's been raining all day. A cold, autumn rain.

I couldn't sleep. Memories won't let me rest. It's like it happened yesterday. But it has been a whole year since Nailka, my 20-month-old son left…

Today on 6th September 2001 is the first anniversary of his death.

We had taken a taxi home, absolutely exhausted again. I had held Nailka in my arms as he kept reaching for the vines while saying "vi-gá-gá." This meant "vinagrad" – grape, in Russian. He'd been using his "father-tongue" more and more, preferring Russian over Hungarian.

Meanwhile, my husband had run to get our older son, Csingiz, from kindergarten.

"Dear, don't be angry at us," I had said to Csingiz when he was the last one to be picked up from kindergarten. I knew that he hated when we picked him up late. "They are operating on Nailka tomorrow, you know," I continued, "so we had lots of errands to run."

My head was killing me. It felt like I was about to collapse if I couldn't go to bed. Luckily there was not much left to do. I had packed the bags the day before. I packed the new pajamas – four of them, ten freshly pressed shirts, five pairs of leisure pants, cardigans, lots of diapers, baby wipes, children's books and a few toys – old favorites and new ones.

I imagined how happy he'd be to see the Tomy Train running around the tracks, and I smiled. But my mind immediately jumped to little Gergő, who used to have the same toy train, and that made me sad. Where's little Gergő now?

It made me shiver.

I also packed two nice colorful bath towels, a hand towel with a bunny on it and lots of other little things. After surgery, in the ICU, we would need the new toys, story books. They would again chain him to the 1.5 meter tall infusion mounts, which he couldn't stand.

Who knows how long the recovery will take and when he can come home? Who knows how long it will be until the family is back together?

I packed lots of clothes because I knew I wouldn't come home anytime soon. My husband, Ruslan, can do the wash with the machine, but I can't expect him to do the ironing too.

I visited the ICU the day before. I was looking for the head of the department to ask permission to stay beside my son during the night after visitation because we had never left him alone ever. This was the main argument for choosing to have the surgery locally, not in the capital. All this was very important to me.

The professor was not in, but the nurses kindly told us that we would have the time to discuss this when we were admitted. They also said that he is very fair and the parents of "oncology" children can expect some extra leniency. But if Nail should need a medical ventilator, I wouldn't be able to stay for the night – they told me.

Oh, my God, I thought. *On a medical ventilator?* And my stomach turned into a knot from the sudden fear.

No matter what happens, I'll stay by his side. They can only remove me by force. We agreed on this with my husband. Not only because we didn't trust anybody anymore, but because we knew that Nail would need us every minute of every day. We had lived through so many wonders together, and we knew that our warm caring love had gotten him through the biggest crises and would ultimately heal him.

We only heard good things about the ICU from the other parents. We had spent half a day there before – thankfully, only due to a misunderstanding. I ascertain that everything is in order, the nurses are well trained, know what to do, and they are human. Just like they need to be. It was a good feeling, encouraging.

We agreed with my husband that if we got permission to stay by Nailka overnight, he'd replace me after a few nights, and from there, we'd be there alternatingly just like we had been during the beginning of his illness.

There were two reasons for this. Firstly: I was not going to last long living on a chair during nights and caring for him during the day, although I already had some experience with that. Secondly, this way I could spend some time with Csingiz – even if late at night – reading, playing, talking like in the good old days. Our recent absence, when our family got torn in two, had already been very hard on him.

Any nights spent at home together were cause for celebration.

The 5th of September was going to be a day like that.

Shameful or not, but I didn't have the strength to even shower that day after running errands the whole day. As soon as Nail went to sleep in my arms, I put him down on the big bed and under a blanket. He slept sweetly on the right side of the double bed where once, long ago, before the illness, his father used to sleep. The white railings had just been installed, preventing him from falling off the bed.

I lay down beside him, and as a habit, I checked every five minutes whether he had slid to the edge of the bed where he could hurt himself or kick off his blanket.

I could still barely hear Csingiz's laugh as he played with his father and whispered a small thank you to the heavens for giving such a good father to my children. Someone who really adores them and would do anything for them.

I tried to recall the events of the last two days, but my head was splitting from a headache.

Early on 4th September, one of our friends Oleg gave us a lift to the children's hospital. It was a great help that this time, we didn't need to spend money on taxis like so many times before. We did not own a car, and since we couldn't take public transportation with Nail, taxis were our only option. We spent more than $1000 on taxis, but Oleg was the only one of our friends to offer his help. He picked us up at 6:15 a.m. because he started work early. This gave us free rides in the mornings but meant we had to spend around an hour waiting in the yard or in the oncology's corridors.

It was cold that Monday morning, so I dressed Nail in a small coat. In his little hat and brand new brown shoes, we walked in the yard hand in hand.

I never let go of his hand because a fall in his condition could have proved fatal. He couldn't walk alone anyway. The tumor in his right ear also damaged his equilibrium. I didn't know, I just thought. Since nobody ever said it out loud.

It was a wonder in itself that he could walk at all.

We walked in circles. Nail was having fun. We chased cats, birds landing on trashcans; we watched the hospital wake up, the doctors arriving one after another, nurses walking in, other patients with their relatives.

When he was tired, he asked to be held in my arms.

Sometimes we would sneak into the corridors to visit the others when we saw they were not sleeping. Other times we sat down on the old plastic chairs of the corridor only to get right back up, on to explore something else.

Aside from being skinny from the strict diet and chemotherapy, he looked just like his peers. His vocabulary was much bigger, though, full of medical terms like koher, syringe, cannula, bottle, sting, etc. He called his favorite – a crocus-yellow plastic cap – "kupa" ("coopa") and was rigorously collecting them. They came in sterile packages, and every time the doctors performed something with the cannula on his chest – like washing, drawing blood, closing – they screwed the old one off and put a new one in its place. Then he would always ask for one for himself. We already had dozens of them at home.

He also learned that if they put a cap on the cannula, it meant good news: he could either go for a walk in the yard or go home.

He was sitting on the examination table on Monday morning and patiently tolerating the exam as the young lady doctor changed the bandage holding his cannula in place. He was gripping the yellow cap in one hand and giving non-stop instructions to his doctor, listing the required equipment: syringe, gauze, cream, cap, HOME…

Even the doctor laughed.

"Thank God, he is having a good day," I said to myself.

We were again sitting in the corridor; I had the results from our daily "finger sting" in my hands and was relieved to see that our blood tests looked wonderful. Well, for a child with cancer…

I was filled with pride and good feelings. Here in this department, the rules are very different from the real world, and these seemingly banal things can define the mood as well as the doctor's tasks for that day. In this microcosm, there is no tomorrow. There is only today, but even that is filled with questions because dramatic turns could take place anytime during the twenty-four hours. This is where I learned to appreciate the wonders of every minute and moment, to be grateful for every hour spent together, for every curious look, every smile, every little word said aloud. Because I knew all of these meant that my child is alive…

Dear God! How much I'd changed in half a year.

I never thought that I could endure all this, swallow so many tears, suffer so many insults, not to mention the pain gripping my soul.

And I still have strength left. I faced the Grim Reaper and turned my back on him to embrace in my arms, to protect the one who is the most important to me: my sick little boy, for whom I'd gladly give my own life.

Around 8:30 a.m., Ruslan arrived. He took Csingiz to kindergarten and then hurried after us. We were facing very important events, and both of us were nervous.

At last, the professor arrived and called us into his office before starting visitations.

"Look," he said, "this surgery is our only chance to fight the tumor. The medicine in the cerebrospinal fluid did not yield results. The tumor did not recede as we had expected. It stayed the same size or may even have grown in the last few months. If we succeed in removing a large enough part of it, then during future chemotherapies, the medicine won't have to get through so much mass to get to the cancerous nodule and kill it. We know that you oppose surgery, and believe me, we don't like to put children through this either."

We just sat and listened. Nail was silently paying attention in my lap. My mind was full of a thousand questions, but a choking ball in my throat did not let me speak. I was close to crying…

It had been almost half a year since we came here. Once, at the beginning of the illness, the professor had once told us that "this is, of course, a fatal disease," but he said it so silently that if we didn't listen to his words as though our lives depended on it, we could easily have not heard it at all.

Afterward we never officially discussed it. Instead of death, everyone concentrated on treatment and healing.

We received the treatments, endured the inhumane side effects, being grounded, the small everyday sorrows, and we cried at every small improvement.

It was hard, but we finally reached remission, which in our case meant that the number of cancerous cells hiding in the bone marrow reduced from almost 100% to below 5%. And without remission, there was no chance for healing. For us, it was a wonder.

When we got to know about the disease, the cancerous cells in Nail's body could already have filled a smaller watermelon. And most of these we could eradicate together.

There was only this walnut-sized mass left, this ball of disgusting parasites, this tumorous formation degraded into an alien body that evaded us.

Yet, its deadly destructive power seemed so unbelievably unlikely.

If only we had more time. If only we could delay this intervention with a scalpel that would cause more suffering and pain for our child.

The professor sighed like he could see into my thoughts. I wondered how many similarly desperate parents he had encountered.

"Unfortunately, we can't wait any longer," he continued. "Nail is now in ideal condition for a surgery, the best possible. This is why we halted the chemotherapy, to stabilize his condition for the operation. But we can't wait long because we risk the diseased cells starting to multiply again. And chemotherapy is not a permanent solution…"

"We are very afraid of an operation. Is there no other way?"

"What else could we do? You oppose radiation as do we, since we're talking about a small child. What's more the ear, brain of that child…" as he helplessly lets his hand fall.

For a moment, I saw the professor as a human, an angry grandfather, who fights not imaginary but real demons of his own. We asked each other many times with Ruslan why the doctors are so alien or even apathetically insensitive. Why couldn't they empathize with us and feel like us parents do?

Probably because this is an awfully hard but noble profession. And few can keep this hidden beauty, to find it and care for it, guard it year after year, decade after decade. To face death on a daily basis, seemingly powerful but often unarmed, helpless, watching through an unmoving mask as the dreams of innocent children cared for through months and years get instantly destroyed by a murderous parasite from inside their own body.

I read in a book by psychologist Dr. Alaine Polcz who dealt with children with leukemia for many years that a head doctor while fighting not to cry once said to a mother: "I know that our pain doesn't even come close to yours, but believe me, if we stacked them together, they would reach the sky."

A beautiful thought, and maybe there is truth in it.

The openness that the author shares with us in the book *A Time for Death* as professional experience came as a shocking discovery. Because I too as an affected parent have lived through many of the same experiences.

"I remember being on holiday, looking on with amazement that there exists another world where children run free, people are happy, angry or sad about little nothings. In sunshine or in twilight children run around on the squares. In the hospital we didn't know what the weather was like outside. In the evenings stepping out, I wondered that it was warm or raining. During the day we could have looked out the window but somehow it didn't come to mind. The outside world was closed to us. We only saw the patients and the work."

Parent or doctor, space got narrowed down for both of them. In my observation, there is only one important difference between them. Healers separate themselves from the physical world mostly because of their work, while the worrying parent falls victim to separation and emotional closeness. They shy away from nearly all community participation. When they realize that their child came to be in the shadow of passing, they have no choice but to live through the loneliness, that dying really is a private matter. Because the real loss is theirs.

I tried to interpret the professor's words. What could be going on inside him?

We decided to go ahead with the operation because it gave a real chance for healing. If it doesn't help and the tumor can't be removed, we won't experiment anymore.

If death wants Nail in particular and touches him with his icy hand, there is nothing we can do but embrace him, caress him, kiss him with warm, honest, unconditional love until his last breath… with us, at home…

"Yes, we have to try this," the professor confirmed. "Look, I don't believe in any other methods, no matter how much the press talks about them. I know the facts, and I will only follow solutions supported by researched, proven statistical data."

A few minutes later, I took the envelope that contained my son's medical records under my arm – the records that were kept top secret since we first stepped into a hospital.

Ruslan remained with the small one, while I was running to the neurological hospital a few hundred meters away to get information from the assistant professor of surgery about our surgery the next day, on Tuesday.

My stomach was reeling from nervousness. I was thinking about opening the folder tied together with a string, looking over every document, looking for something, anything that could be important. Why don't we have the right to know all the facts, to see clearly? As I was sitting in the corridor, I held the folder closer and closer to me as if my life depended on it. The envelope in my hand became wrinkled and dirty from the sweating of my hands. I was unbelievably tense and tired. There were many adults waiting, some of them (the "return customers") greeting the nurses in a friendly manner, although I was sure none of them had a cancer patient son waiting for them in another hospital. I had plenty of time to think about our only meeting with the assistant professor of surgery. It was less than three weeks ago.

We waited for him in the hospital, in our room – Nailka, Ruslan, and I. It was early afternoon, a few slivers of light darting through the strip curtains. We were preparing to go home after our daily treatment.

One of our doctors, the professor, was on his one-month summer holiday after a year of exhausting hard work. After many decades of healing, he had recently been promoted to professor. He dedicated his life to healing children with cancer.

Another one of our main healers, the female adjunct, had just came back and taken over managing the department.

She talked to us too and filled us with optimism with her calm remark that an operation aimed at removing parts or the whole of the tumor would greatly help Nail's chances of recovery.

She had consulted with an excellent neurosurgeon, and she wanted us to get to know him and listen to his opinion too.

A smiling, middle-aged man arrived wearing a suit, sleep deprivation and exhaustion immediately apparent on his face. He excused himself for being late, saying that because of the summer holidays, he was now acting manager of the Neurology Clinic, having to deal with all the important matters. Once he was done with us, he had to immediately go back to his patients.

He examined Nail and told us that he had already seen the images of the tumor and found that an operation was absolutely justified and urgent.

Upon my request, he told me that they would make the incision behind one of the ears – an everyday routine penetration for them. It is from there that they would start the exploratory operation. What he sees then will determine the next steps since he can't know in advance what he will find under the microscope.

"You know, until I make the incision and see it with my own eyes, I have no basis to form an opinion," he said. "I will make a decision about the further course of the operation based on the facts, namely how big a part of the tumor I can safely remove. What's most important is to make sure that the tumor is not hemophiliac, but I can't know that until I've started…"

"So if it starts bleeding, what will you do?" I asked, startled.

"That's my prerogative. There are certain professional methods…"

"Oh, Barbara." The female adjunct tried to ease the sudden tension. "I've been a doctor for twenty years but a child bleeding out in the OR. I've never seen something like that. Stay calm. Talk over what you've heard, and try to make a decision as soon as possible. We will not be offended if you choose to seek the help of another professional."

"Why would we do that? You consider your colleague one of the best, don't you?"

"That's true; he's an excellent surgeon."

"Doctor, I'm really scared about this whole bleeding tendency. I'm not a professional. What happens if the tumor starts bleeding? Isn't that too risky with such a weak blood test?"

"Don't worry so much, Barbara. We'll take the necessary precautions. We'll find and order irradiated red cell concentrate for him and if needed platelet preparations to support coagulation functions. During the operation, Nail will receive a constant drip of blood to compensate for the unavoidable blood loss. As soon as he can be transported, we'll send an ambulance to bring him back to our ICU and monitor his condition."

"Are you sure that I'll be allowed to stay with him during the night? I don't need a bed; a chair will do. This is our only condition."

The adjunct did not refuse. "If there are no complications, I'm sure you'll be allowed to stay. They may even be happy that you'll be keeping a constant watch; the personnel there won't be able to do that. Doctors and nurses have to monitor many patients."

"Well, if you agree with us, then let's not delay anymore. Please start organizing the details."

So our time has come. Maybe tomorrow we'll know more about this damned tumor that has been ruining our lives for the last six months. We hope it'll give the doctors more insight into how to modify the therapy, the so-called chemotherapy protocol. If they know more about the enemy, they will be able to better defend against it, and that seemed encouraging.

The door opened, and I handed over the envelope with the medical records that were so protected from us like they had been secret FBI files.

But come on: Nail is my son after all. My signatures are needed; I'm the one taking responsibility. How can I possibly make a decision if I don't know anything?

"Please, come in." The door opens before me.

"I have reviewed the material and looked at the images," the neurosurgeon says. "I'm not sure that I should be the one doing the operation. The tumor, it seems, is separate from the cerebellum. It touches and pushes on it but only the surface. What's for sure is that we'll need an otolaryngology specialist. Without one I cannot operate. The ear is not my field of expertise. I suggest you go back to the children's hospital and discuss this with the professor. I will call him later."

I can barely contain my disappointment. I want to cry.

"So, there won't be an operation tomorrow?"

"Absolutely not. I think the otolaryngologist will want to take a look at the child before."

I'm climbing two steps at a time. I huff-puff. I'm angry as hell. I've had enough of the whole healthcare system. I'm outraged that I have to go back and forth between two institutions like a postman, with a secret package, for absolutely no reason.

They wanted to operate on my son tomorrow, and instead today, they decided to use a different professional. Not the one who's been looking at our case, our son for the last three weeks; not the doctor whose expertise is well recognized by everyone; not the one we chose, the one we put our trust in.

This is madness!!!

I walk back to our usual spot and tell my husband the news. I take Nailka into my lap, and we wait for the professor's news with more bitter feelings, in vulnerable uncertainty that will determine my little child's fate and future.

It would be so good to cry a little. But I mustn't. I can't seem weak in front of my son. Where will he find strength? How can a twenty-month-old child hold on to a weak mother?

The professor arrives with good news:

"We can't operate tomorrow, but we can do it the day after. I've spoken to the otolaryngologist; he's a well renowned, knowledgeable professor, incidentally my neighbor. It is fortunate that he accepted the operation because he knows our story; he's seen all the medical records. I can't think of a better professional. I'm very happy about his decision. Before you go home today, please wait until I compile the images. I'll also write him an official letter. Tomorrow, take the records to his hospital just like you did today with the neurologist. Go right on the ground floor; they will already know you're coming and will take you to the professor. He will obviously examine Nail. Meanwhile, we'll order the blood needed for the operation."

That night at home, Csingiz was looking at one of his favorite picture books about the Titanic. Nail had already been bathed, and now he was lying beside his brother half naked pointing at the pictures saying: "Tita… Tita…"

Ruslan and I looked at each other and smiled. We were very proud of our children and the fact that they loved each other so much. At last Csingiz had some time to calm down and see that he too had a family: a mother, a father, and a brother, just like before. It has been six weeks that, thanks to the adjunct lady, the four of us could spend all afternoon, evening, and night at home, together. We went to treatments as outpatients.

It was an unbelievably great gift, one that can't be expressed by money. After all those cruel and desolate months, we could finally live our lives together as a family. In peace, like Nail's disease never existed. Everything now seems so far away… Everything bad, everything that hurts… It's the calm before the storm…

We really needed this short idyllic time that filled us with the nicest hope of all, the hope of life. We could again dream of sunshine. In truth I never for a moment believed that death could come into our home and take Nail with him. Some dreamy illusion made me think that we were somehow different from others. But deep inside, I always felt death's breath on me. I felt it as it made the hair on my back stand, as it reveled in my most paralyzing fears. They fed it, sustained it, and despite their intentions, they made it my prisoner. I became indebted to it.

As the months passed, it became increasingly clear that soon it will be free from the tyranny of my shivering mind.

I naively thought that I could silence it. If it appeared with its ghastly silhouette, I closed my eyes, so I didn't have to look. If it started playing its sad tune, I covered my ears not to hear it. If it started jumping up and down in front of my eyes not hiding its true nature, I just turned my back on it.

It was easy to silence it, blind its stabbing stare, avoid its hurrying steps. All I had to do was not to accept its existence. I questioned my own predictions and premonitions.

These were trying times. We lost two four-year-old little fellow patients in less than a week.

Since then I fled from the hospital whenever I could. With Nail in my arms, I ran as fast as I could… far away.

Did I do it to defy death? I don't really know. I wanted to show that we were still alive.

I tried everything to wash the stain of cancer from my son. We lived only in the present, we healed, and we loved each other in every moment.

On Tuesday our first stop was the otolaryngology.

At first, Nail was sitting in my lap, but quickly getting bored with the monotonous waiting, he started wandering around the rows, looking thoughtfully at some chairs, and then trying to climb them. The other patients in the waiting room looked at us as though we came to the wrong place.

They soon called us in. The professor gave the impression of a short-spoken, considerate man, a little more like a scientist than a doctor, sometimes lost in thought. He examined Nail. Then with an incredulous look on his face, he stepped into another room and called in another doctor much older than him. They both agreed it was a strange case, not one they'd ever seen during their practice.

They observed a yellowish-white pus node looking mass that covered many of the known organs and was doing unbelievable damage in the process. The eardrum was not visible at all.

I closed my eyes, and I remembered a scene from the movie Alien. Only there have I seen such a yellowish goo that ate away at the characters' organs like acid. All of them died. I wonder what pH that thing had and if there was something that could neutralize it.

The professor's voice brought me back, and he looked at me thoughtfully. There was something inexplicably unsettling about it.

From here we went back to the children's hospital, to a small building in the yard, to have Nail's blood checked. We got the results in a few minutes from the sample taken from his fingertips.

At least that calmed me. Nail's blood tests came back as excellent – considering the circumstances and his cancer.

"Well, this looks excellent," our doctor said. "With a blood test like this, we don't need to give any blood. But we'll take a sample and send it to the blood bank, so everything will be ready for tomorrow's operation. We'll order two units; that will be more than enough until he gets back here. Please wait for the visitation. Then go back to the otolaryngology, and see to the hospital admission."

Before we left, they called us in to bring Nail back to the examination room because something had happened to the drawn blood, and they needed to re-take the sample, this time from a vein. This was the third time they drew his blood that day. Nail was sitting on the examination table and crying. He was utterly bored, and he held on to me crying continuously.

"Mom, Mom, Mom." He looked at me desperately, but I couldn't do anything for him. I just squeezed his thin arm and angrily watched as the needle pierced his vein and started to fill with his blood.

I felt guilty because I, his mother, could not protect him from this painful, suffering inducing, barbaric world.

I resonated with him. I felt as the needle entered him, but the needle pierced my heart instead of my skin.

I felt like a nobody. Like a helpless wimp who's unable to revolt to protect her child. I became a ruler without power who can't bring the much-needed peace to his people. I was a grave without flowers whose desolate view isn't even worth a look.

No matter how I try to transfer the pain from my little son to me, I can't even do that. I just keep hugging him warmly, softly, to assure him of my love without having to use words.

If everybody spent just half a day here in this department worrying for the fate of their cancerous children, the world would look very different. It's a place where words get new, real meanings, words like "important, inconsequential, many, few, tears, smile, reality" and "illusion." And hate can be overridden by love in a few short moments.

We got into a taxi, and we traveled to the location of the operation to see to the matters of hospital admission and surgery preparations.

I did not understand why the routine had changed. Why didn't an ambulance take us there together with the ordered blood like before? In my experience, the final examination and surgery preparations had always happened at the children's hospital.

I didn't like this running back and forth.

As the taxi drove us through the busy inner city, Nail happily greeted every statue we passed. This put us in a somewhat better mood.

When we got there, the doctor on duty told us that the professor did not intend to examine Nailka again, since he already saw everything this morning. We couldn't even meet him. And I really wanted to ask a lot of things because I knew nothing about the duration and technique of the operation, nor its possible complications, aside from the bleeding mentioned by the neurosurgeon in August. I wanted to know whether appropriate precautions had been taken to avoid it.

"Doctor, did the two units of blood for my son arrive from the blood bank yet?"

"Pardon me?" He looked at me questioningly. "We are not equipped to store blood here. Look, we only have this one fridge that our patients use to store their food."

I looked over the long corridor, the overstuffed patient rooms. Not long ago, it was over 100 degrees hot. And this man suggests that for the several dozen patients there is only one fridge?

I grimaced, and then asked him to look after it. Make sure that the blood arrives in time for our operation in the morning.

"Oh, you're not going to be operated on in the morning. The boy is fourth in the schedule. That means he won't get in until 10 a.m., so you only need to arrive around seven."

"You mean we can go home now?"

"Yes, yes. Once we're done with the admission."

"Are you staying with him?"

"As far as I know, none of us are staying. After the operation, he'll be transferred to the ICU of the children's hospital."

"That may be the case tomorrow, but we're admitting him today. So let's think and come up with a nice disease for you."

"Is this really necessary?"

"This is the easiest way for everyone. For you most of all since – anything can happen during the treatment – you get to stay with him during the night."

"I see."

"Is the child sensitive to any medication?"

"I'm sorry, but did you not get his case history?"

"We did, but it's probably with the professor."

"Oh, that's fine. So, he's sensitive to Ceclor (aka Cefaclor, an antibiotic) and Asparagine – he went into an almost fatal anaphylactic shock from the latter after one of his chemo treatments. He can't receive that and any of its derivatives, but I don't think you use that kind of thing here."

"So, Cave Celdor, Asparagine," he repeats out loud. "How did his illness start?"

"This March, he had to go to the hospital because of long fevers accompanied by sudden, sharp pain. Later they detected a tumor in his right ear. They treated him as an acute lymphoid leukemic, with chemotherapy, because his bone marrow was also affected. There were no pain attacks since then. They suspended the treatment ten days ago to allow his blood to recover. I almost forgot. Here's his blood test from earlier today. You'll probably need this. You know, I always ask for a copy for myself. I'm collecting them."

"Okay, my colleague will make a photocopy of it."

"If you don't mind, may I ask something?"

"Please."

"How will you know tomorrow morning whether he's in condition to be operated on?"

"Look, I know nothing about this. They informed us at the children's hospital that the child is in good general condition. They confirmed this in writing."

"I see," I said, sighing.

"Please also sign this," the doctor said as he pushed another form before me.

The form read:

"Declaration: Based on the information given to me about the nature, possible outcomes of the operation I hereby accept it to be performed on me/my child/my ward."

Under it: date, two witnesses, still unfilled.

I'd ask, but why bother? It's no use.

I take the pen and sign it.

"Good, we're almost done, and then you can go home," the jovial young doctor says. "Just one last signature here, please."

I'm reading the text:

Consent form where I declare that XY doctor had sufficiently informed me about the following:

1. Intracranial tumor

2. Recommended treatment: middle ear surgery

   Its possible risks:

   – flow from the ear, face-, nerve and muscle weakness, paralysis

   – bleeding, numbing of the tongue, loss of taste

   – infection, dizziness

   – permanent eardrum perforation, tinnitus

   – damage to the oscilles chain, partial loss of hearing, ear canal infection, inflammation

   – medicine oversensitivity, permanent loss of hearing/deafness

- damage to the chewing joints, insensitivity of the skin around the operated ear
- pain upon chewing

"Good God, these complications are all possible?" I ask at the brink of fainting.

"This is not everything; we have to add two more items to the list upon the professor's explicit request. You'll need to sign these two items separately."

He slides the piece of paper in front of me, which in written letters reads:

- rupture of the major head artery and varicose veins
- death due to blood loss

"Doctor, why do we need this? Is this really possible?"

"The professor must at least find it realistic if he asked me to write it down here. Were you not informed by anyone about the possible complications? Look, some of these are no big concern, but we have to write them down. Others, on the other hand, pose a real, serious risk."

"But… all this?" My eyes start to well up; I can barely talk. "So, his face may get paralyzed, he can go deaf, bleed out, get infected? We were told that this is a routine operation, that they won't risk anything and only remove as much from the tumor as is safe. Because this is only the first step, a sort of exploratory surgery. They said risks will be taken in the second step in case this one yields no results."

"I'm sorry," the doctor says. "My task here is to have you sign these papers. This is how we always do it."

"Yes, yes…" I mumble dazed and sign the papers.

I don't even register as the doctor says something in Latin and tells me he's found the perfect diagnosis for me. What do I care in this condition? They could write me up with cancer too if they want.

"They made me sign to confirm that I understood the possibility of lots of complications," I tell my husband.

"Okay, what?"

"That he may become paralyzed, deaf, or even die…" I whisper to him, not wanting Nail to understand what I'm saying.

"What? Do you know what it's like when someone's face is paralyzed? Are these people mad? And you signed it?"

"Yes."

"Look, Barbara, we may have to call this off. We may have to reject the operation."

"But you heard too that they think this is our only option."

"Right. For fuck's sake."

"Ruslan, they are the doctors, after all. They are the ones that need to know what the best solution is. Not to mention, what we would say to the professor at the oncology if we rejected the operation. Who will treat him then? If we make them angry, where will we continue the chemotherapy?"

"I don't trust them. Just look at this department. Best we get out of here as soon as possible."

"They supposedly have a well-equipped operating room, and afterward, they'll transfer Nail to the children's ICU."

We went home, and I collapsed into the bed beside Nailka. I was asleep in seconds, forgetting the outer world, patient records, complications, the whole operation. In my dream, I was running around the lake again. Sometimes I glanced at the surface; it was murky. I couldn't see the bottom. I was just doing my miles like someone was chasing me. I was drenched in sweat; my legs felt like they were made of lead. I could barely lift them off the ground. I felt a strange metallic, salty taste in my mouth like I was swallowing my own blood. I had no saliva left. My mouth went dry, and my lips started to crack. I was completely exhausted and insanely thirsty. Even the sun was baking me, its rays blinding me more and more. I just keep running on and on… but my strength is leaving me, and I don't see the goal yet…

Suddenly I am awoken by Nail's crying. The realization hits me like lightning – this is reality. I am no longer asleep.

"What is it, dear? Does something hurt?" I fumble around for the switch of the bedside lamp. I glance at the clock; it's 11:30 p.m. Outside there's only darkness and silence. Csingiz and Ruslan have been woken by the crying too.

"Did he throw up again?" my husband asks.

"No, thank God. He must have had a bad dream."

"Mom, Mom, Mom…" Nailka keep calling to me – "Ke, ke, ke…"

"Of course, dear, here's my hand, my thumb, of course. Just keep squeezing it, my precious, the "light of my eyes." How would I let you go? You know I love you very much, don't you?" I kiss his cheeks.

I'm looking on as, holding my finger, he slowly shuts his eyes. His fear is slowly leaving him. His breathing becomes more and more regular. Finally, he slips into unconsciousness, sweetly dreaming, and I carefully free my thumb from his grasp. Interestingly, he can only go to sleep while holding my thumb; he won't accept any other finger. I tried to fool him before; he did not fall for it. It seems strange that he woke so suddenly without any reason. He never usually does. Most of the time, he sleeps through the night although recently we woke up many times because he felt sick and threw up.

Every time he was asking for my thumb or as he called it "ke" (hand).

My thoughts took me to the hospital, and I was thinking what our doctors would think if I said I had to stay with him during the night because he can only go to sleep with my thumb in his hand. I smiled. This is what doctors will never understand. What it means to be a mother in this situation. How can I explain to them that I can only sleep well if I feel him squeezing my thumb and hear him breathe?

My thoughts shifted from the doctors to next day's operation. It woke me up completely. I took a shower, drank a glass of water and sat down on the couch in the living room. I don't bother anyone here with the lights. I was remembering the day's events, and I wanted to cry. I could finally do it. Never in my life have I been so afraid.

I tried to remember my father's words as he had visited me a few days before:

"Listen, Babi. I don't know how to tell you this, but there is something you need to know… Nail will die! During the operation, something will happen, but I can't see clearly what…something will be missing. But don't cry; they'll bring him back. If only I know what will be missing. Everything hangs on this. Give him all the medicine they prescribe. Don't forget because that may cause him to die. Something will be missing. But of course, he'll come back. Don't cry. Forget I said anything. Everything will be all right."

"Nail, what's the matter? Why are you crying again? What happened? Shhhh, I'm here with you. Don't worry"… I run back to the bedroom. "It's okay. You barely slept half an hour."

"Mom ke, Mom ke…"

"There, here's my hand. Take it. Squeeze it. You see? I'm here. I'll climb beside you and sleep with you."

What could have happened? I barely close my eyes, and Nail starts crying again and again, every twenty minutes.

At around 2 a.m., he starts again: "Mom, Mom, Mom, ke, ke, ke…"

"Calm down, baby, please. You really should be sleeping. Tomorrow will be very hard for us; you'll need all your strength. We won't be able to wake up tomorrow when Oleg comes and takes us to the operation. We'll be very tired."

Unexpected, he starts crying inconsolably. What could be bothering him? Oh God, please help me! I sat up, held him close and started rocking him. I inserted my thumb into his flailing little hands. I put my hands delicately around him, and we cried together…

"It's okay. It's okay. Everything is fine. Here's my hand. I love you, Nailka; I love you so much…"

My body is shaking from crying, and in a moment's time, an ice cold shiver runs down my back. I cover him with my kisses and repeatedly whisper to him: "I love you, I love you, I love you, my little son, and I will always, always love you. You know it, don't you? Always, always, forever and ever and ever and ever until the world ends… I will always love you."

He slowly rests his head on my chest and starts to get silent. I lay down beside him, and we sleep until the morning, our hands intertwined. But deep down I feel: this is much more than that… a handholding that lasts eternally.

Then I turn to my half-sleeping son and whisper to him: "My baby, I know you are a special soul. A very wise soul… I want to learn so much from you. Please, get better and teach me."

I'm looking at him through a veil of tears, and it's like I can see a faint golden aura around his head. Well, let's sleep It looks like I'm starting to hallucinate.

As Nail sees the black car in front of the gate, he shouts: "Ole, taxi!" and it eases the tension a little.

At the bottom of the small street leading to the kindergarten, Nailka notices the foiled yellow jeep with a "Jumbo" sign painted on it. He almost jumps out of my lap he's so excited.

"Jee, Jee" he keeps repeating.

"Yes, dear, that's a jeep," I answer.

We drop Csingiz off at the entrance to the kindergarten; he kisses his little brother as a farewell. He's hesitating. It seems he wants to say something. Then, finally he whispers: "Don't worry. It's not going to hurt…"

Then he grabs Nailka's thin arm full of needle marks and adds: "I'll come to you and bring you a nice gift. We saw a really sweet one with Mum last time; you'll like it."

There is silence the rest of the way. We listen to Nail as he tells us about the different colors of the traffic lights.

At the hospital, Ruslan says goodbye to Oleg with a handshake. They both look ill at ease.

"So… call me if you need me," our occasional taxi driver says.

I carry Nailka in my arms; my husband is walking beside us with the red sports bag and one filled with food. It's full of his latest favorites: the life-giving, homemade brown bread, purified water, and grapes. He wasn't allowed to eat and drink since last night, and now he's demanding his dues.

"I can't give you any, baby. We have to wait some more. When you wake up, you can have them all. I wish we weren't fourth in line. Then I could feed you sooner…"

Nailka becomes silent, surrendering to his fate.

"Look how smart he is," Ruslan says. "He knows, he feels something's going to happen. When he can't eat, they always take him into the OR. See, how silent he is?"

He takes him from my arms and kisses him. Takes off his cap and coat, while I'm going over to announce our arrival.

When I get back, Ruslan is standing in front of the window with Nail in his arms. I can hear him teaching the colors and the makes of different cars. Many people are arriving, looking for a spot in the parking lot. They are both pointing fingers when I get near them.

At this moment, a silver minivan rolls into the parking lot with a huge black cross on its side.

We look at each other with Ruslan. Then without any words, we stagger to the opposite wall. Like a maniac, I grab Nailka from his arms and hold him close to my heart…

He's silent. He's sitting so still that he almost melts into my hug, with a distant look on his face. He feels that something bad is going to happen to him… Strangers in green coats are coming for him and taking him to the OR. They will poke him with cold instruments, and neither Mom nor Dad will be there to protect him and keep him warm.

A nurse passes us by with an encouraging look on her face, stops, turns back and says: "Oh, such a cute little boy! Tell me, are you always this good?"

At last the doctor from yesterday arrives. He greets us and tells us that we won't be able to meet the professor today because he's been in surgery the whole day. Around ten, it will be our turn.

"Doctor!" I shout after his departing image.

"Yes?"

"The blood. You know, what we talked about yesterday. Did the two units arrive for my son from the blood bank?"

"I don't know, but I'll look into it soon."

"What does he mean, he doesn't know?" my husband says, but only I'm there to hear it.

"Maybe they've already taken it into the OR," I say, thinking aloud. "It needs to be stored at room temperature before use."

The doctor comes back after a few minutes.

"I've spoken to the professor. The child won't receive blood during the operation. They only ordered them for storage," he says.

"Excuse me? This can't be. There must be a misunderstanding. Nail needs that blood. You saw his blood tests. You know he has leukemia. They promised us at the children's hospital that he's going to receive blood during the operation."

"Possible. But according to our professor, it won't be needed. And afterward, he'll be transported to the children's ICU. Anyway, the blood bank is just a few meters from us. If there's any complication, we can get the blood in less than ten minutes."

"I see."

"Ten minutes can be a very long time when there is trouble," my husband says angrily. "They're screwing with us."

The nurses are handing out the breakfast from little carts. They kindly offer us some, but we shake our heads in refusal. Only Nail's eyes light up when seeing the bread, and he starts to ask for it:

"Ke… ke…!"

"No, Nail, I can't give you any," I burst out, this time with tears in my eyes.

"No appetite? Don't worry; it's the same with all parents. But you'll see. Everything will be okay," the nurse says, smiling.

I look at her gratefully because I'm getting very nervous. The rooms of the OR open and close many times. They are taking patients in and out. Soon it will be our turn.

A few minutes before ten, the neurosurgeon who will assist during the operation dashes into the department.

"You see? Everything is organized here," I say to my husband, who is now visibly agitated.

The adjunct nods, having noticed us as he enters a door.

Then an assistant steps up to me and tells me in a harsh voice to take the sweater off the child.

"I'm sorry. I thought you'd take it off him inside, so he doesn't catch a cold," I mumble.

He doesn't answer.

Nail starts to cry uncontrollably, and I notice the signs of panic in myself. My adrenaline spikes, my stomach curls into a ball as I try to clumsily take off his sweater. Never before has he cried so hard. I feel like my heart will break in two.

Meanwhile, the anesthesiologist gives me another paper to sign, and I – to be sure – ask him whether they know that Nail has a central venous catheter (CVC).

"No, I didn't know," the doctor smiles. "But we would have noticed it sooner or later."

"I'm just saying, so you don't have to poke him needlessly. You know," a tear rolls down my face, "they used to poke him a lot, but since he has the CVC, it has become much easier."

"I see."

"Will you be using that milk-like stuff for anesthesia? They used that last time."

"Probably."

"You only need to take off that little yellow cap and attach the anesthetic. Please don't put in a new cannula if it isn't necessary."

"All right, we'll try."

The grumpy OR assistant returns and is impatiently milling around waiting for me to hand Nailka over. These are hard moments. My son is using all his strength to hold on to my neck and incessantly cries, "Mom, Mom, Mom…"

He doesn't want to go, and some strange, frightening instinct whispers to me not to give him to the assistant.

But common sense is victorious once again.

We're watching the doors close behind him, fidgeting with our hands. His loud cries become more and more silent and then disappear completely. Ruslan swears and is rubbing his eyes. I slump down, cry, and start to pray silently.

Minutes passed that seemed like millennia. We stood, we sat, we paced back and forth in front of the OR. Nothing.

How long can it last? They told us that it could be anywhere between thirty minutes and ten hours…

At last, the doors of the OR open.

The neurosurgeon steps out in civilian clothing. I glance at my watch: it has barely been forty minutes since they took Nail in.

The adjunct absentmindedly starts toward the exit; my husband runs after him.

"Oh, I'm sorry," and he shakes Ruslan's hand. "Congratulations! Everything is in order. They'll soon bring the child. The strange thing is that we didn't find any tumors. Only a node filled with pus."

"Really? This is fantastic." I squeeze my husband's hand.

My joy is without boundaries. At last, I can blurt out my question: "Tell me, doctor, did you remove much of that node?"

My question takes him somewhat by surprise. He hesitates and then answers pensively:

"I would think so, yes."

"Thank you, doctor. We will contact you again."

"Oh, it won't be necessary." He waves his hand and then leaves.

"Why do you think he said that he 'would think so'? Maybe he hasn't seen it? It's not important. What's important is that Nail's fine. He's not paralyzed and not deaf. We can stop the chemo because his marrow is in remission.

A few more weeks and we can go home. This is wonderful. I suppose he'll get some strong antibiotics to stop the inflammation."

I let out a big sigh. Suddenly, I'm as happy as I can be. I feel like I'm a bird flying up to the sky, to heaven. I can see Ruslan feels the same. He hugs me and says: "We'll tune him up, get him strong. In a few years, we can forget all of this. Is it really possible that he'll be a basketball player? He'll be dunking in the NBA."

We stand in front of the OR like soldiers. I can barely control myself not to go in to see my son and hold his hand.

After ten long minutes, the door opens. They roll out the bed of our son with Nail inside. He looks terrible.

"Oh, my God! Are you sure he's all right?" my husband asks the anesthesiologist.

Nail lies there, still, with white face and white lips. The turban-like gauze dressing on his head completely soaked through with blood.

At first look, he looks dead, but I can see him breathing.

"He lost a lot of blood." The anesthesiologist turns to us, "but there is no need to worry. We monitored his condition and checked his blood during the procedure. We were able to use the CVC; we also closed it with heparin."

I feel suddenly moved. There lies my beloved child not 2 meters from the OR in this war refugee camp they call the ICU. The beds are separated by curtains; there are no doors in the room, only doorframes.

No instruments are turned on; they just put him in a small, plain metal bed. His face is ashen; he does not react to anything. And they dare say he's all right. I don't understand.

"Try to wake him," the anesthesiologist asks us, but first, she tries to wake Nail herself.

"Wake up!" she lightly slaps his face and pinches him.

Before she leaves the room, I turn to her.

"Please, doctor. You said that he's lost a lot of blood. We can see it too. His lips are white. Shouldn't you change the blood-soaked dressing on his head and send for the blood?"

"Look, his white lips can be caused by many things. The dressing on his head is a covering dressing, which means it's the second layer, and we can't take it off. As for the blood – we can't order it. That's the professor's duty."

"Then please tell him. Call him here."

"We can't. He's currently operating."

"Please, call the ambulance immediately. We need to take him to the children's hospital."

"Okay, I'll go and call. Please calm down."

I'm very afraid and am suddenly filled with sadness. I step to him and stroke his face and hair as much as the dressing allows it. I do it carefully, slowly, not wanting to cause any pain. He's breathing but not like he usually does. I say his name, but he doesn't react.

"There must be some problem here," I tell the nurse, who is barely twenty years old.

She brings an instrument and tries to put it on one of his fingers. The oxygen meter shows a figure of forty; then the adult clip slides off Nail's finger.

"Please call the professor; he was the one who did the operation. Say something, for God's sake."

"All right, I'll try."

"Look, nurse, blood is seeping from the dressing." I pull off his socks, and his sole is white too. "He needs blood immediately. His HTC values (hematocrit) must have fallen very low. If the dressing didn't cover his ear, we could see that they're white too. Look at the edge of his lips; they're like chalk. What are you waiting for?"

"Oh, you know so much… They don't pick up the phone in the OR; the professor's mobile is busy as well."

"Please call the emergency ambulance at once, or my son will die. Is there not a doctor in this fucking hospital?" I scream.

The nurse starts to cry: "I'm not going to cover for anybody…"

The anesthesiologist appears. She's still completely calm; she wants to check on Nail's condition.

"Did you call the ambulance?"

"What? Oh, yes, yes…"

"Look, doctor, since you left, I tried to wake him, speak to him, but he doesn't react to anything."

"How come? Let's try together."

We slap his face together; she slaps him harder than me.

"Baby, Mom is here, Mom. Can you hear? Mom is here. Nail, wake up, please. I love you so much, my little son."

The small body moves, gathering all strength he tries to sit up. He spoke to me in a rattling, yet strong voice, and turned to face me.

"M – o – m!!!"

I felt the happy calm in his voice that he knew I was beside him. He was happy I was there, and he recognized me. Like he was waiting for this moment for a long time.

This sole word he spoke contained everything that matters, that's important. Fulfilled wish that I was there, yet a deep sadness. He was saying goodbye to me. There was some questioning blame, clumsy obedience in that word, like there was someone rushing him from a distant universe, from the eternal empire of the infinite. He looked at me deliberately. There was gratitude, wisdom, innocence in his big warm angel blue eyes. He was no longer afraid.

In a moment, my mind became clear, and it became apparent that I would soon lose him.

But not yet. While he was slumping back to his pillow, he kept his gaze on me. He and I became one in an intimate symbiosis.

In these few fragments of a second, I lived through the realization of unconditional love, something that most people can't experience in a whole lifetime. This fleeting moment was just for us. The secret contact of our consciously chosen togetherness made in nothing, everything, eternity melded us together in unity. I saw as the glimmer went out of his eyes as he slumped back onto his pillow making it bloody.

His face turned away from me, and the realization instantly hit me: The light of my eyes is gone.

The nurse ran to him and tried to measure his blood pressure. The adult cuff, of course, just slid off his arm. My husband stepped toward us and told that he had not managed to find a single doctor on the corridors.

The nurse asked for immediate emergency help over the phone.

I feel like I will die. I give up everything we've been fighting for. My strength has left me.

I take Nailka's ice cold fingers into my sweaty hands and am calling to him: "I am here, baby. I am here. I'm here with you, Nail."

The anesthesiologist and a nurse in green suddenly burst in, the child cuff needed for taking blood pressure in her hand. Where has this been until now?

It reads 40/10, but in the next moment, it starts drawing that line. The doctor gives him central oxygen and then runs off to hurry the ambulance. It has been more than twenty-five minutes since her last call to them. In this time, ten ambulances should have come…

"I'll run into the OR to the professor," says the nurse.

"Let him know that I'm 0RH positive just like him. I'd like to give him blood if possible."

The doctor arrives running. I tell her that Nailka's breathing is irregular, and his blood pressure can't be measured.

"I'll get the anti-shock gel that will help him." My husband is still searching for doctors.

I have been left alone without any help with my dying child. The helpless, rattling, unable to speak patients watch our battle from a few meters away.

If I were in the Sahara without any food or drink, I wouldn't feel as alone as I feel right now. Panic slowly seeps into my bones. I try to calm myself. Like an asylum patient, I just shout to myself: "What should I do?"

At this moment, Nail's body contracts. His jaw snaps shut, his head turns stiffly to the side. He's not breathing.

I try to force his mouth open, trying to prevent his tongue from slipping into his throat. I can't. I'll never forgive myself for not becoming a doctor.

"He's not breathing, he's not breathing!" I shout and burst out into the corridor. "We need a doctor now!" My eyes scan the surroundings, and at the end of the corridor, I glance at a white coat.

"Please, please, did you hear an ambulance arrive? Where is that damned car? My son is dying, and he's alone in the patient room… His jaw is locked, and he's not breathing."

"I work in the labs," the calm answer comes. "I can't help you."

"Bah!" I say angrily and run back to Nailka. I pull off his blanket and try to strongly massage his sole; maybe I can get some life back into him.

They all come through the door at once. The anesthesiologist with the Gelofusin infusion, my husband with the department doctor and the nurse without the professor.

"The cap needs to be taken off again and replaced with the riggings," I speak in shock.

"Hold this." They put the infusion bottle in my hand.

"Oh God, they still have to do the venting, or he'll get a pulmonary embolism, and drain the heparin from the cannula," I mumble to myself.

My hands start to cramp up and shake. I hold the bottle high, but my whole body is shaking.

The doctor covers Nailka's face with a dark gray mask. The nurse steps to me and takes the bottle from my hands.

"Please, leave now. Leave!" They order us out.

They grab the cart on wheels and start with it back to the OR. The doors open, and they push my son back in. Then a middle-aged man with a stretcher arrives.

"Where is the patient?" the paramedic asks.

"In the OR," I answer.

He rushes in after the others.

After him comes his colleague, the second paramedic from the ambulance.

"Excuse me; do you have oxygen in the ambulance?"

"I'm sorry?"

"You came for my son, and he needs oxygen. Can I come with you in the ambulance?"

"Sorry, but I don't know. I don't think so."

I turn to my husband and tell him: "You should stay here until they remain here. I'll take a taxi to the children's hospital because I want to be there when the ambulance comes. Come as soon as they transfer him."

Ruslan nods looking defeated, and I run to the nearest taxi station.

I jump into the first one and shout to the driver to drive very, very fast.

The distance must not be more than 2 kilometers. Traffic seems slow as a snail.

I pay the driver in front of the building and jump out of the car.

My first stop is the oncology. I desperately rush into the kitchen to the nurses where they are serving lunch.

"Where is the professor? Nailka bled out, and we don't have the blood."

"He's not here. He's in the OR."

I run off to the ICU in the other building. I climb two stairs at once. I push on the bell for the department like a maniac.

"The ambulance is coming with Nail," I say quickly to the nurse. "He lost a lot of blood, and he didn't get any to replace it."

I want to give precise information to help the preparation of the nurses.

They are very conscientious. They immediately send everyone out of the department, and they start the preparation. Only I don't hear the sirens – the ambulance doesn't come.

There must be a big problem. He may have already died, I think to myself.

I instinctively start running downstairs; maybe I can meet one of the paramedics on the yard and get some information. When I step out the door, I see our professor and run after him.

"Professor, professor!"

Finally, I catch up, and he stops. Meanwhile, I crash into an electric box with full force, but there is not time for that. I hurt my arm badly, but I don't take notice of it.

"Professor," – I'm panting – "there's a big problem. Nailka lost much blood and did not get transfused. We don't have the blood. His jaws locked, and they took him back into the OR. The ambulance arrived half an hour after they'd called for it. They should be here by now, but I don't see them anywhere."

"How can that be?" he asks wonderingly. "I spoke to them not long ago over the phone, and they gave me good news. They told me the child's condition is stable."

We hurry back to the ICU together where he immediately starts dialing the hospital.

They make me sit in the kitchen where I can clearly hear everything he says.

"I see. So, you're reanimating him. Of course, he'll only be transportable afterwards."

He dials again, this time the blood bank.

"Yes, its XY from the children's hospital. Yesterday, we ordered two units of blood for Nail Haszjanov. Please immediately send one to the otolaryngology and the other one here. We don't know yet where he'll be. They're currently reanimating him."

He hurriedly starts to go somewhere, but I'm faster. I ask, looking into his eyes:

"How is he?"

"They're trying to revive him now. The ambulance will only bring him if he comes back..."

So, it's true. It isn't some kind of joke. Nail is really dying? This isn't a joke?

"Professor, please be honest. Can they still bring him back?"

"Well, it depends on how big the blood loss was..." His expression turns thoughtful.

"It was big. He lost a lot; I saw it with my own eyes. His lips were as white as your cloak..."

Clear speech.

I'm running, but I don't know where. I'm waiting, but I don't know what for. I'm confused. My actions are governed by instinct; shock guides my footsteps. At last I run to the phone booth near the department of surgery. I'm unable to use my phone card correctly. I try again. And again. Nothing.

I go into the department, straight to the nurses' desk.

"Please," I start. "Can I use your phone? I think my son has died. I'd like to call my mother."

"Yes, please wait… We'll ask for a line out. But who is this about? Is he our patient?"

"It's little Nail from the oncology. He's only twenty-months old. They performed lumbar puncture on him right here almost weekly."

"The center's busy. I'll try again."

"Thank you."

"Oh, I know who it is," says a woman. I never knew what her job here was, but I didn't like her from the start. "You know, he was very sick."

I want to beat her. What gives her the right to speak of Nail in past tense? Nobody has said anything officially. I run off, confused. Everything is foggy; my head feels dizzy.

In the yard, I meet a young female doctor who'd treated Nail for months.

"Come on, let's make you a nice strong coffee."

I refuse.

Upon returning to the oncology, I meet some familiar people, but I'm unable to talk to them. I feel desperately lonely. The news about dying insulated me.

"Do it silently," some people whisper, "not in front of the children. We don't want panic in the department."

Szilvi, the cleaning lady, hands me her mobile phone: "Use it if you need it."

I look at her gratefully.

"Mom," I say in a defeated voice. "They are reviving Nail. He bled out."

"Oh no!" my mom screams. "That can't be. I'll be right there."

"No, don't come. I don't even know what I should do, where I should go. Stay near the phone. I'll call you."

Answering machine on the other number. Laci and Gyöngyi, the naturopath couple, aren't at home.

"Hello, it's Barbara. Nail is being revived. Please help. Do something so he'll come back."

I slowly climb the stairs to the ICU. I don't know what to do. The ground has slipped from under my feet. I slump down onto a char. I have no idea how long I've been sitting here. My gaze is fixed on the window. Maybe I'll see the ambulance, hear the siren.

A nurse steps up to me and asks me if I'm all right.

"Where's the professor?" I ask.

"He left with our own professor. They drove to the other clinic to help revive Nail. I think they might need you more there than here…"

"You're right. I left my husband there alone."

I take a taxi back. I find my husband standing in front of the OR, his eye fixed at the ground.

"What happened?" I ask.

"I don't know. They didn't tell me anything."

"Since then?

"Since then."

"Did the blood arrive?"

"Not yet."

The doctor from yesterday who made me sign the "formalities" confidently steps out of the OR.

"Is he alive?" I ask.

"Of course. His functions can be maintained. He's receiving heart massage."

At the end of the corridor, I see a man hurrying. He has Nailka's two units of blood in his hands. I look at my watch. It's 1:25 p.m. They have been reviving him for 130 minutes. Can anybody survive this long without blood?

My mind makes two more desperate attempts to drive death from the room. I start to hope: he will come back. The blood is finally here. And my father said it too: he'll come back, and everything will be fine.

"Ruslan, did anyone ask for me while I was away?"

"For you? They probably don't know who we even are. Nobody has spoken as much as a word to me…"

"I meant about my blood. To donate. Didn't they ask for me?"

He shakes his head.

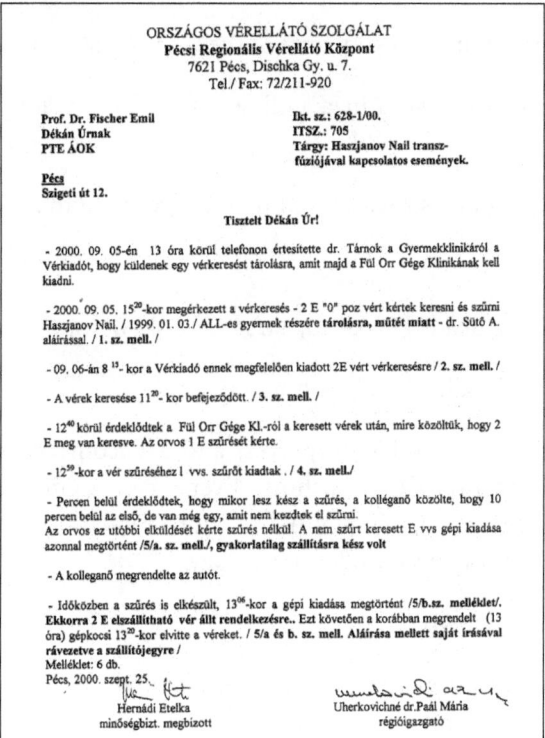

Weeks after the tragedy, we received this transcript from the blood bank "accurate to the minute."

"The scumbags!" he hisses. "They left him alone. I haven't found one damned doctor in the building. When I caught this one," he points at the department doctor, "he hadn't been breathing for seven minutes. Where the hell was his blood? I told you that they were going to screw it up, but you didn't believe me. You gave them a chance. And now? What good did it do? Where is our son?"

My husband – like me – is on the verge of madness. He could kill somebody right now, but he's controlling himself.

I start praying. Asking help from the Virgin Mary again. In an instant, I feel like a hundred year old woman.

The OR opens, and they start stepping out one after the other. I glimpse a bag of unopened blood in the hand of a man in a green coat. I instantly realize that what I feared the most has happened. We lost our child.

"Did he die?" I ask silently.

"The professor will inform you," one of them says, not looking at me.

"It's over," I say to Ruslan in a hollow voice. "They stopped trying to revive him."

We wait for ten minutes silently, and then the room of the OR opens.

"Please, come in…"

"Did he die? Is he dead? He's dead, isn't he?" I shout into the nothingness.

"Well. Well, yes. Yes, he died." He bows his head.

Everything blurs in front of my eyes, and I become dazed. My body becomes an uncontrollable machine. Everything seems dreamlike and distant. My stare is rigid, my mouth dry. I don't remember how, but I make it to the window where they offer me a chair.

Ruslan doesn't sit down.

My mouth becomes automatic, and an alien voice from inside starts repeating: "I can't stand it. I can't stand it. I can't stand it. I can't stand it…"

Many people are standing around me, but the faces become blurry. The professor's voice reaches my ears as if coming from under water.

"He was very sick, you know, but we did everything. We couldn't bring him back. We saw no point in continuing."

"He can't be dead!" I reply, but half-mad, I still give him respect. In truth I want to scream, "You're lying," yet I don't do it. Although I lost my dignity a long time ago, I rock back and forth on the chair like a complete madman.

"His brain is still alive!" I try to push them. "Bring him back. He's in a coma, isn't he? He's very strong. He'll come back. Try it, please. Use some electronic device. Don't let his brain die."

"He's dead, his brain too." The professor shakes his head. "There is nothing to do."

My husband is fighting his tears back, using his broken Hungarian accusingly: "Where was blood? Why did you say to us that there would be blood? Would my child be alive now if the blood was there?"

"Well, yes, yes. I don't know," the professor says looking at the floor.

"I want to see him." I jump from my chair.

"No, no, you can't. The OR is a sterile environment. You can't go in there."

"We will," my husband stresses. "We want to see our child."

"Come this way."

I walk on tiptoes not to disturb his dream. Some follow me silently.

And there he lay on the operating table.

On his left side, naked. Like he was resting.

At the end of his feet a diaper. A blood filled tube coming out of his mouth. His eyes were open, rigid, without light. I want to pick him up, take him into my lap like long ago. Feed him, care for him, kiss him. To warm his bold, broken body in my arms. Hug him close to my chest to let him hear the beat of my heart… but all is in vain. So, this is what a human life is worth?

I want to run away with him. Far away from civilization.

We start crying together with my husband, our pain flaring up together. A deep, convulsive shaking washes over us. We can't believe Nailka is gone.

"No, no, no…" is all we have the strength for.

Somebody touches me and leads us out.

The cleaner can resume her job beside the body of our beloved son.

The professor is waiting for us at the door:

"If you excuse us, we must leave. Back to the children's hospital to the other sick children."

Chapter 2
NIGHTMARE AT THE CHILDREN'S HOSPITAL

It was the 20th of March 2000.

The call reached me at our office supply store in the inner city.

"Come home quick. Nail is very sick. He has a fever, he's coughing, and something hurts him a lot. He won't stop crying," my husband said with worry and anger at the same time.

"All right, I'll call a taxi and head home right now."

I wonder if it's really a big problem on the way home.

Ruslan tends to see things magnified when they concern our children. He reacts with panic whenever one of them gets sick. Nailka has been sick for weeks, a mild flu. He's coughing, sometimes has a little fever but nothing more. He takes his medicine prescribed by our family doctor, he eats well and is in a good mood. He's already teething; he has at least twelve of them now. If it hurts him too much. We use Cataflam, an anti-inflammatory to ease his pain.

In the evenings, the four of us play together. I only get home around 6 p.m., so we make the days last longer to allow us to spend more time together. The children almost never go to sleep before 11 p.m., and we have the time to get up at around 9 a.m. We can do it because Csingiz still goes to kindergarten, so his schedule isn't fixed yet. By the time he's in school, I, hopefully, won't work until the evenings. By that time, the business we just began will start up nicely, and I will be able to dedicate more of myself to my family again.

Nailka is taking his first steps. He can be very amusing. He's quite chubby – 12 kgs (or 26.45 pounds) – so balancing can be hard for him.

We gave him a big sofa where he can practice safely. And at the end of it, we shout over each other and make it a competition to lure him toward us, to see whose arms he will land in. Most of the time, of course, his brother wins. He stands above all.

Csingiz is very proud of this. Many times, he simply calls his brother "Baby." Again and again, he leads him back to the starting point at the end of the bed, then gently lets go.

"Te… te…" Nail happily screams. In his language, it means brother (tesó). Then he starts stumbling forward again.

When they get tired of running around, we build towers as big as them, which Nail is happy to knock down afterward. Toys are flying toward every corner of the room. Bathing is an extra relaxing time. Finally, I too can sit down if only on a small chair. I watch from next to the bathtub as they splash and play together.

After, we take them out, wrapping them in bath towels. I carry the small one into bed while the older one is handled by his father. Storytime is also part of the evening rituals. Then after some snacking, they are visited by the sandman. I look at them for a little while more, our little wonders, the true meaning in our lives. We draw our strength from them, we live for them, we fight our everyday battles for them.

I whisper my secret wishes into their ears. I started with these little spells when Csingiz was a little baby, about six months old.

"Be happy, live long. Be successful, rich, healthy, lucky and satisfied. Mother will always love you," I whispered for years.

Somehow it doesn't quite work with Nailka. An unknown force, a voice from nothing, always crosses me and leaves me with a bad feeling.

I say to him: "Nailka, be happy. Live long."

He answers: "NO! NO! NO!"

He argues with me.

Inside, I scream with all my might: "Get out, get out of my way! I'm ignoring you. You are nothing. You don't exist to me! Know that Nail will be happy, lucky, healthy, and he *will* live long."

All the while, he staidly keeps saying: "NO! NO! NO!"

Because of this, I recently stopped doing my evening prayers. I'm waiting for this frightening stranger, this monster to disappear. I hope it will get bored if I keep ignoring it.

I paid the taxi driver and hurried to get inside the house. Nailka was half lying, half sitting on the arm of the stroller. He let out big sighs and looked very sad. I had never seen him like this.

He'd been crying for hours; that's what exhausted him. Ruslan and my aunt tried everything, but he could not be appeased. Looking at him, it was clear that his fever had weakened him like some kind of drug, and he didn't even have enough strength left to cry. He was just sighing and moaning.

I forced myself to calm down, took him into my arms trying to make him feel safe. He looked at me gratefully but started to moan complainingly again and again.

I called our pediatrician while trying to take his temperature.

She left her full office and arrived in a few moments. At first glance, she knew that something serious was going on.

"His temperature is 39.6 C (102.5 F)," I told her "I just took it, but I already gave him a suppository earlier."

"I'll give him an injection to ease his pain. Barbara, I have to be honest. I have never seen such an intense pain in my life. And I've been a pediatrician for many years. You'll have to go to the children's hospital to get him checked. We can't exclude the possibility that he's swallowed something."

"Yes, but that never happened to him before. And his fever is also going down."

"Still, you have to go in for observation. It will be better this way. I'll call them in a moment. You're in luck. Today's doctor on duty is a very conscientious lady. I know her well. She'll do every test needed to exclude him swallowing something and aspirating."

Csingiz started to cry. He didn't want us to go. I told him there was no need to worry. We'd probably be back tomorrow…

The taxi took us to the stairs at the entrance to the hospital. I hadn't yet gotten out of the back seat when a young doctor stepped up to us, smiling: "Is he the baby we were waiting for? Did he choke on breadsticks?"

"I'm sorry? I don't think he choked on anything, but we'd like to be sure. So far we don't know why he had inhuman pain and such a high fever."

"We're going to the ICU. Soon the head doctor on duty will be here and will examine the little one."

It was already dark outside. There was only one other baby in the ICU right opposite us. I could clearly see him through the double glass walls.

Meanwhile, Nailka dozed off. They brought him back from the examinations. They took a blood test and X-rayed his chest. I was waiting for the results. The injection had obviously worked – he no longer seemed to have any pain or fever.

I sat on a chair beside his bed and held his hand. The phone not half a meter away from us went off loudly more than once. Then he woke and cried. I tried to calm him and help him get back to sleep.

Nail is sleeping in an alien environment, surrounded by strangers for the first time in his life.

The doctor steps toward us with a worried look on her face.

"We have the results, and they don't look good. Do you have knowledge of any hemophiliacs in your family?"

"What? Oh God. No, of course not. I don't know anyone like that. Why?"

"Because it can be inherited. Your son's blood test indicates a very serious disease. We have to stay alert during the night. He might need medicine or some other kind of intervention. Just to be safe, we'll insert a canola into his arm so we can act fast if we need to."

They woke him and brought him back into the examination room. I was fidgeting with my hands at the door. My head was spinning from the absurd looking thought that Nail could be hemophiliac. How is it possible that no one noticed it before?

I heard him crying, but I was unable to do anything. What's more, I was becoming agitated.

I decided that I would stay with him. I read that I had the right to do so. I'd insist on it, no matter what.

After the procedure, they put Nail back into his bed. The nurse on the night shift started tying his hands to the rails on the bed. I protested. Nail desperately tried to sit up and asked me, sobbing, to take him into my hands. We made a compromise with the nurse: I let her tie up one of his hands and took the other one in mine. I held it firm as promised, not letting him grab the catheter from his wrist.

Spending the night on a chair seemed to make it very long. I managed to sleep for a few minutes, resting my head on the rails of the bed. My shoes started to feel too small.

I'll ask Ruslan to bring me slippers tomorrow. They probably won't let me take him home tomorrow, I thought to myself.

It was almost dawn, and I had to go to the toilet because I hadn't had the chance since last afternoon. But I couldn't use the ones in the department because those were reserved for staff and patients.

"Look, I could let you into ours, but the head doctor would kill me," the nurse informed me.

"But how would she even know?" I asked.

"I'm afraid to risk it. Please use the one in the clinic. Today we're on duty, so in theory that door there and the restrooms beyond it should be open. It's not far, just a few minutes. You go down to the ground floor, step out the entrance, go down the stairs, go through the yard toward the left, and you'll find the entrance."

Meanwhile, Nail was thrashing around on his bed, so I didn't want to leave him. Then we'd have to tie both his hands. And at any time, the loud phone beside his bed could start ringing. It's set to maximum volume, so the nurse can hear it even if she's reading in the kitchen, resting, or chatting in another department. That's a consideration. After all, this is just an ICU, not a sanatorium. The child will get home sooner or later. He can sleep at home.

It was a very cold night. So, now I'm supposed to put on my thick coat, cap, everything, to stumble around in the darkness looking for a toilet when there's one not 2 meters from me? This is absurd.

I held back the urge and waited for my husband to relieve me in the morning. Next day, they repeated Nailka's blood tests. He could make stool in the meantime, so I stuffed two vials with referrals with it as the doctor on duty had asked me. I gave the little boxes to the nurse to pass them on to the National Public Health and Medical Officer Service.

We hadn't encountered a doctor in the morning, so I had to hold my feverish child in my lap. My husband stayed with us for a long time. We could get nervous together because nobody informed us of anything. In the afternoon, the lab results arrived, only there was no one to explain them. At least I supposed they had eliminated hemophilia because they were talking about suspecting thrombosis and, in my non-expert opinion, I thought they were opposites. The doctor on visit who didn't care to greet us simply called her colleague from last night "stupid."

"Such a nice place…" I whispered to Ruslan.

"Ah, bullcrap," the head doctor continued. "It's only a virus, nothing more."

"But what should we write on his chart?"

"Virus… infection. That's it."

And she walked out. She probably thought we had heard enough.

Nail barely ate. He started losing weight. I had medicinal formula prescribed for him, which had always helped before when he had diarrhea.

On the shelf behind his bed, they allowed a room about 20 centimeters wide to store our things. There was no nightstand of any other storage. He was throwing up, so I had Ruslan bring in a few sets of clothes, two bottles, and some toys. Not many things, only the essentials.

They told me off because I had made such a "mess" in our 20 centimeter zone. I promised to return some of the stuff tomorrow.

We didn't receive any attention after that. Next time I saw a doctor was during the evening visit. A different (but still grumpy) head doctor was not happy to see me there. What's more, she became angry.

First, she demanded to know from the nurse on what grounds I was still there.

"They allowed me here the first night when we came in," I answered with indignation.

"Why don't you go home? Why are you sitting here?" she asked rudely.

"Because I want to stay with my son. I am his mother."

"Uh huh. And you, of course, want to be an "A+ mom," don't you? Is an A not enough?" she said with supercilious contempt.

"I'm not going home."

"Why do you think you're needed here? You don't trust us doctors? Do you want to monitor us? Put on your clothes and go home. The child will sleep through the night. You can come back tomorrow."

"He won't sleep through it because he can't sleep from the constant phone ringing. And there's no way I'm going home. Don't even try to send me away."

"No harm will come to the child from spending a few days away from his mother. Why do you need to play the martyr? I'm telling you for the last time: go home!"

I was fighting my urge to cry. I wanted to say something very nasty and offensive, but I swallowed my anger.

"Look," I said, snarling, "according to Hungarian law, I have the right to stay by my underage child and nurse him if I don't disturb the hospital staff by doing so. I insist on exercising my rights, so please stop insulting me."

"Oh yes, your rights…" she waved sarcastically. "If we get a new case during the night, you'll have to go."

"By the way, if you're curious about my son's condition…"

She turned and, without saying a word, walked out of the room.

It was a good visit.

We could barely sleep during the night. Nail had the hiccups, I tried giving him some hospital tea to drink, but he either spit it out or threw it up. He cried often, and I had to hold him in my lap during the whole night. At dawn, he finally went to sleep.

Thank God, I could get my biological needs sorted out during the afternoon because the nurses warned me that the door to the clinic wouldn't be open as this will not be the institute on duty. This way I could only relieve myself under the stars. I made the necessary precautions and drastically lowered my fluid intake after lunch.

On the rails of Nail's bed, I too could get a few hours of sleep using his pullover as a pillow.

I woke up in the morning with a queasy stomach, hearing the voice of the doctor from last night.

"She'll give up sooner or later. She only has herself to blame."

Well rested and with a wide disdainful smile, she managed to wake Nail up too: "So, Mom, did you sleep well?" she asked

It seems she couldn't give up such an easy opportunity.

"Yes," I said exhausted, and a tear appeared at the edge of one of my eyes.

Nothing of mention happened the next day. They looked at us during visits, but sometimes this too seemed unnecessary since it was only a small viral infection.

They did not touch on the topics of why his bloodwork wasn't improving, why his fever wasn't going away, why he still had diarrhea and threw up multiple times daily despite the fact that he was getting modified antibiotics several times a day directly into his veins.

Nail still wasn't eating, and it was bothering me. We couldn't give him any food from home, only hospital tea in his bottle. He was refusing it, almost crying. I didn't understand; he loved to drink tea.

When I didn't see anybody near me, I took off the cap and tasted the tea in the bottle. In the next moment, I was already wiping it off the floor because I spit it on the ground as fast as I drank from it. It had a horrible bitter taste.

I didn't care if they told me off for drinking from it. So when Nail fell asleep, I went out to the nurses' kitchen with the bottle.

"I'm sorry, but why didn't you ask me to bring sugar and lemon for my son's tea?"

"Why do you ask that?"

"He hasn't been drinking from it for days, and now I've tasted it. I think this should be drank by the person who made it. I won't give this to my child anymore."

"Why? What's wrong with it?"

"Taste it."

"Oh, I know what must have happened. They must have mixed it up with the other tea. The one we use for gastric lavages. We get it in the same looking jugs. I'll bring you some of the other type."

"I'd be delighted."

From this day on, Nail got the sweet tea that he liked to drink.

It was maybe the third night where Nail's moaning woke me from my snooze. It was quite similar to the one on the night where our doctor sent us here. The moans were not so intense, but he was obviously in pain.

I waited for a while, but when he didn't get better, I had the nurse call the doctor on duty.

She did come, but there were no thanks in it. I probably woke her from her best sleep.

"I don't think this is moaning," she said when I told her what had happened. "I think he's just sighing. He probably has a stomachache. Give him a No-Spa," she ordered the nurse on duty.

Not an hour later, Nail's condition worsened. His fever got higher and didn't go down even after using a cold pack. The pain also became worse. He was moaning louder and more desperately. We tried holding our ground with the nurse on duty, but a little while later, this time she offered to wake the doctor.

She didn't at all like that I was right and the child was in real pain. She examined my son in a way so that she didn't have to look at me. She only spoke to the nurse.

"What's this child sick with? Why is he here in the ICU?" she asked the nurse.

"Because of a viral infection," the answer came.

"They don't know what's wrong with him." My mouth slipped.

"Why do you think that?" she asked angrily.

"Because they haven't told me anything."

"Well, I'm sure they know," she snapped at me superciliously.

Only because I'm not a doctor, this didn't make me feel like a complete fool.

"Has an otologist (a hearing specialist) seen him?" she asked the nurse.

"No," the answer came.

"He should see one. Give him a milligram of Algopyrin (a medication to reduce pain and fever)."

During the morning, I nervously stood in front of the examination room at the otologist. An assistant took Nail from my arms and into the examination room shortly after which he started to scream at the top of his lungs.

I stepped to the doorframe while a burly assistant stood in front of me on purpose so I couldn't see the procedure. I got very angry because I wanted to see what was happening to my son. All I could see was that the doctor pulled out a bloody needle from Nail's ear.

He punctured it. I thought. *He shouldn't have done it without my consent. He was not allowed to do that.*

The assistant suddenly closed the door on me. I felt my position very humiliating and unjust. The doctor didn't even take the time to speak to me before he acted. Without considering the consequences for the future. Without properly finding out what he was poking.

When the door finally opened, I hurried to my son to console him. He was still crying loudly. I was caught completely off guard by the doctor's accusations: "What did you stick in this child's ear?"

"Excuse me? Nothing. Why would you assume that?"

"Look, you damaged the child's eardrum. Do you use ear sticks?"

"Yes, but only inside the auricle."

"Then somebody else did it. Does he have a bigger brother?"

"Yes, but he doesn't stick ear sticks into his ear."

"Then he must have damaged it with a sharp toy or something."

"I find that impossible. We would have noticed it. We never leave the children without supervision."

"Look, Ma'am," he spoke to me, this time in a stronger voice to give the words weight, "the eardrum inside the child's ear has been damaged. This is a fact. Do you understand what I'm saying? Something covers this damaged eardrum, so I can't see it well. It's filled with fluid. I have just drained a lot of it. Some alien object is in your child's ear. I'll look at him again tomorrow."

"Could this cause his perpetual bad condition and bad blood tests?" I asked devastated.

"That's not possible," the doctor answered.

During afternoon visitation, my husband found me crying. I could barely tell him about the events. He immediately agreed that Csingiz couldn't have stuck anything in Nail's ear, much less unnoticed.

Meanwhile, due to the four day and night long wait, my feet have swollen up in my shoes. I shuffle down to the bathroom and wash my feet. I can barely put on my slippers. My feet are as red as fire, and I can almost feel them burning. I can barely stand.

Nail is already playing in his father's lap. My husband is a big man, sporty, easy to anger with somewhat crude manners. Interestingly, no one is bugging him. They don't point out when he takes the toys from the shelf and doesn't put them back in the exact same place, or when he reaches into the fridge for our own water, or when he leaves Nail's bottle unwashed…

"I'm so exhausted Ruslan," I tell him. "I don't know how much more I can take."

The night passed uneventfully. My feet were hurting unbearably, but I managed to get a painkiller and a piece of cloth I could wrap them in. One of the nurses gave me a tube of anti-inflammation ointment. I looked at her thankfully.

"It looks really bad," she said. "You could get a thrombosis any time. You can't play around with this anymore. Why don't they let you use one of the empty beds? Wait, I'll get you a chair so at least you can elevate it."

By morning I'm neither dead nor alive. Somewhere between the two. In my mind's eye, I can only see a soft bed and a hot bath.

At last after five days, they finally let me know who the department's head doctor is.

Well, they could have told me before. I have, of course, seen the crude mannered female doctor around. She was the one who called her colleague stupid, and today I heard him say the same about a young bearded doctor because he had set the suicidal girl's IV drip wrong. She had been right that time, by the way.

Despite all this, she must be a good professional or she could never have made it this far.

The next time she reaches for the phone near us, I take a deep breath and say to her: "Doctor, sorry for bothering you, but what's wrong with my child?"

"He's shitting himself, and blood also looks like shit."

"What did you say?"

"That his tests are coming back quite bad."

"Could I know some details? What's wrong with him? Why are his lab test results not getting better?"

"Well… I don't know." She kept turning her head like she was doing some muscle relaxation exercises. "He must have some kind of viral infection. We're still doing tests. Be patient."

Meanwhile, the head nurse comes in and notices my swollen feet.

"Now I personally forbid you to stay the night. Your feet look very bad. You'll get a deep venous thrombosis, and we'll have to admit you too. There's no point in this."

"Yes, I agree. I can't do it anymore. I need to get home before I collapse. I thought we'd be home in a couple of days. My husband will stay with him tonight. I've already talked to him about it."

"Promise me you'll go to a doctor. In the meantime, buy some good ointment in the pharmacy. How long have you gone without sleep?"

"I've been sitting on this chair for five days, but sometimes I could get a nap in on the edge of the bed. I thank you for worrying, but I'm made of strong stuff. A mother caring for her child can't become sick."

In the afternoon, Nailka has diarrhea again. I try to find out if they already completed testing his stool from the previous two days.

The nurse looks at me perplexedly when I ask her.

"You mean the samples the head doctor tossed in the trash? We didn't send those to the labs. So you're waiting for those results in vain."

"But what you're saying is unbelievable."

"Well, it's the truth. The head doctor said that the department finished last month with a 10, 000 HUF deficit (the equivalent to $34.47 US), and we can't allow ourselves to conduct useless tests."

"I'm going to go mad. I'm literally going to throw up from what you just said. So, you want to save expenses on a stool sample? While keeping the patient here in the ICU?"

"Nobody understands why you're still here. They aren't doing anything to him. Maybe because of the capitation."

"Because of what?"

"You know, the money that Social Security pays after each patient."

In the afternoon, my husband and I decided to buy and distribute some gifts. Maybe those will help somewhat. We left the head doctor out. I couldn't bring myself to do it, especially after what had happened.

I'm looking for favoritism over the phone. I've never done it, but now I feel I really need the help since Nail's condition hasn't improved at all. They're treating his symptoms, but nobody knows the underlying causes.

The days start to melt into each other. Sixth, seventh, eighth… They come and go one after the other without anyone speaking to us. We still know nothing at all. They don't even come in during visitations; if somebody does, they turn smiling and exit.

"Naïve little virus, they thought. Harmless," said the infection specialist in the department.

Almost everybody thought that Nail had no serious problems, that he only caught a cold or a virus, no matter how we tried to explain that this was something more. I couldn't give them proof. I only had my mother's instinct, my sixth sense, my looming dreams.

The diarrhea got worse in the evening. The loose, foul stool kept repeating every ten to twenty minutes.

By morning the head doctor allowed the taking of a sample. This time it didn't land in the trash but got sent to the labs. How many days had we wasted? Six, if I remember well, but it's Friday, so they'll only get to it on Monday.

"Touch the diaper carefully," the head nurse warned the others. "It looks like salmonella to me. And that'd at least explain a lot of things."

I wish I could meet the "A+" doctor now. I'd tell her that they'd be "A+" doctors if they already completed all the tests and found out what the matter is with my child. Or at least told me that they failed to diagnose anything so far.

During the night, Nail's catheter slipped out of place. It had been replaced several times, each time inserted into a new vein. No matter that his hands were tied to the rails of the bed; it still slipped out. Worried, I called the nurse. I had every reason to do so.

Not two hours before that, the same thing happened to a three- to four-year-old girl. It took the doctor an hour and a half to put it back, and the girl was screaming all through it. When they brought her back, her blood pressure was over 200.

I wondered if they will stumble around Nail the same way.

I tried to calmly assist the work of the doctor and the nurse to help us get out of here faster. But after the fifth poke, I was thinking about leaving behind my principles, taking my child and leaving. All the veins in his elbow were popped by now, no matter how he turned the needle after piercing a vein or missing it completely. I saw that the young doctor was embarrassed, but he tried to compensate by never poking the place recommended by the nurse. She too was already drenched in sweat.

After forty minutes of watching Nail suffering, the doctor decided to replace the catheter to the same place it slipped from – his wrist. Well, that solved it. Hallelujah!

They covered Nailka's little arm with a bandage so I could finally hug him close and calm him. I was still trembling from nervousness.

"You saw that he never pricked the spot I recommended. That vein would have been perfectly fine. Such an unsure man," the nurse whispered to me angrily.

The weekend passed without events and without progress. They used Smecta to calm Nail's diarrhea. During Monday's visitation, to our great surprise, the head doctor announced that on that day, after ten days of hardship, we could go home. Not that we wouldn't have loved to go home, but we didn't know what to make of it. Nail's condition has only worsened, and they couldn't tell us why.

The results from the stool tests came back and suggested Rota virus infection.

The head doctor let us go with the following words: "At last we found something. It doesn't explain his bad CBC (complete blood count), but at least it's something factual."

My son had a fever over 39°C (102.2°F) multiple times a day, which they treated with Algopyrin (aka Metamizole). He became smaller, paler and lost his appetite. Besides the diarrhea, he also vomited and signaled with small moans that he was in pain. He could keep almost nothing down, and only the infusion protected him from dehydration. His blood tests suggested a critical condition – he could need urgent attention at any time. The otologist who punctured his ear multiple times without any good results also forgot that he had to check up on him on Thursday. We haven't seen him since.

And they want us to go home despite all these?

We had already packed our things when, after eating a nice portion of formula, Nail projectile vomited on everything including his father. It even shocked the nurses.

Afterward, they made sure we didn't leave. They passed Nail over to the department of infectious diseases with regard to his supposed Rota virus.

Before we left, the jaded old grumpy cleaning woman entered. At first I thought she was a relative of the head doctor because the similarities in character were so apparent. But it seems she was just a stone-hearted accessory of this department.

She never said hello and didn't bother her whenever Nailka wanted to sleep. There was not even a spark of empathy or goodwill in her. She ordered me to go outside.

I answered that I wasn't going to leave my crying sick child for thirty minutes until the floor dried, but I'd stand up so she could clean under my chair.

This made her flip out. She threatened to tell on me to the head doctor for not letting her do her job – a threat she kept.

I hated this whole misbegotten system that made it possible that in the ICU of a children's hospital, a rude old hag could order me around without minding her own business.

Her stare was burning. In her anger, she kept shoving furniture around because she saw that I wasn't going to put Nail back into his bed nor get out in my fear of her.

Nail and I hugged each other. We melded together. I used the back of my hand to wipe away a tear from the corner of my eye and then kissed his little head. We shut the noisy and looming outer world, and my dear son went to sleep with his head on my chest going toward a better, more humane world…

He was walking slowly, carefully through the paths of his dreams, and I held him tighter with his every breath the way only a protecting mother can.

This was all I could do at that moment. It wasn't much. But for him, it meant the world.

Peace in a war that's raging inside and outside, a blinking light in the dark silence of the night, a warm touch inside an icy avalanche.

The embrace of souls, dance of grains of sand in a universe without space and time.

An unceasing bond with eternity summoned from the distant past.

A fact-like conviction that we belong together forever, and there is nothing that could tear us – mother and son – apart. Nobody can enter our secret symbiosis that's our armor, our common aura, our joint force field. No mortal can.

In the afternoon, we walked over to the department of infectious diseases. After ten long days, this was the first time Nailka could breathe some fresh air, even if only for seconds.

We got a room on the right side of the corridor, toward the end. The 2x3 meter big room that looked like a cell, with its curtained door, was like freedom for us after the inhumane conditions of the ICU.

Because near the railed metal baby bed was one made for adults. And as part of the room, we also had a little table and a small sink available to us. I could put the toys on the window sill, and our bag with the clothes and hygiene products could fit nicely under the bed.

I was also given a small lockfast closet with a hanger just 5 meters away from the room. And we had a fridge and a toilet as well.

We had to pay a daily fee of 400 HUF, approximately $1.38 US dollars, but three meals per day were included. Most of the parents didn't stay for the night; therefore, it was a favorable solution for adults sitting next to their children often for months.

Moreover, once I caught a phone conversation between the head doctor and the Child Protection Institute. He called them because there was a little boy who no one had visited for weeks. The head doctor made strict rules for his department.

Visitors were not allowed to enter, and the parents were forbidden to bring food. Every time Ruslan arrived, I went outside to the garden to give him enough time to spend with his son.

Beside him, just Csingiz, my mum, our great-grandma and Aunt Marika came to visit. We waved them through the window. A few days later, we had some great news: now we were allowed to take short walks in the garden. That was such a delight!

Nurses and doctors were much friendlier here. They were nice to us except for one nurse. She reported me for feeding my child homemade food (potatoes with parsley and yogurt) and answering a call from my husband. Both were considered forbidden according to her own terms.

I didn't use the canteen because I couldn't leave my son unattended as the canteen was located on the top of another building. Even if I was hungry for hot food, there was no one to ask to bring it here. So I chose to stay next to my son. By this time, he had been hospitalized to such an extent that he jumped into my lap screaming every time he saw someone in white or heard the door open.

The head doctor informed us that the Rota virus is the least serious problem that we could expect. (Nail's diarrhea stopped.) He suspected a more severe cause in the background, something that might explain these bad lab and blood test results.

He was thinking about Epstein-Barr virus, often referred to as mononucleosis. Mono is a serious disease. It requires medical attention for months, but it's curable. He performed a few tests to rule it out.

I asked him about the missed otology control; however, Nail kept moaning and touching his ear. They managed to arrange a visit with another otologist. He was an elder, a practiced expert.

After the examination, he said that he detected strange things inside the ear. The blood filled cyst that had been pierced a few days ago now seemed a polyp-like formation with the size of a lentil. And this was just the tip of the iceberg.

"The cyst is encapsulated and totally covers the eardrum. We need to X-ray it," said the otologist.

"This is exactly what I've been asking for days, but someone here at the ICU said that they don't X-ray ears."

"I don't know who said that, but we'll take radiograms today."

After the X-ray, they held a consultation. The operation was considered necessary, but it was too risky to perform it here.

The head doctor of the department of infectious diseases asked for permission from the director of the hospital to perform an extraordinary CT scan in another institute. Without connections, this would've taken weeks.

This is a very expensive medical examination – at least, this is what I was told – and it is performed only in exceptional cases.

The next morning, we got into a minibus and traveled to another institute just a half a kilometer away. I don't know why, but the head doctor of the ICU came with us. Besides the driver, there was an anesthesiologist since during this medical examination, Nailka needed to lie still, which was hardly imaginable.

My husband was sitting in the back seat. We were tense and silent all the way there.

I was wondering whether we should go to Szent László Hospital in the capital city. I'd already requested that my son be placed over there. The doctor on call told me that we could ask for an ambulance for the transfer and that we had to take the complete medical documentation with us.

I was planning to start this unpleasant conversation to ask for the documentation, but events turned out differently.

We took a seat in a small crowded waiting room. In the middle, there was an old lady lying on a wheeled hospital bed. We didn't know if she was alive or not because she was just lying there motionless with her infusion not dripping any more.

I told a nurse about the infusion. She smiled at me and opened the valve.

I looked around, and I felt I was on death row. I smelled the unmistakable scent of hopelessness.

The head doctor told me to try to put Nailka to sleep. That way we wouldn't need anesthesia. It was the first time she addressed me in a kind and empathetic tone. Shame, that it had a price.

I was standing proudly beside my son as he was lying on the examination table, sleeping. CT scan is basically an advanced version of X-ray.

After the examination, we got back in the minibus. Nail was sleeping still in my arms. We were waiting for the head doctor. As she was trying to step inside the vehicle, she got her bun bumped into the upper edge of the doorframe. Not her head, just her pinned hair. She began swearing, which made us feel very unpleasant.

Between two obscene expressions, I asked about the results. My voice was trembling.

"Oh, yes. The child has a tumor."

"Excuse me! What does that mean?"

"You'll be informed at the clinic."

I thought I was going to die. My husband wanted to know what she said. He was impatient and puzzled. But I couldn't say a word.

It was like we were in a burlesque scene. Everything seemed so unbelievably unlikely. No, no. It can't be true... It can't happen to us... Can't happen to Nailka.

We were sitting beside our sleeping son's bed when the head doctor entered our hospital room.

"I'm very sorry," he said. "We've found a tumor in the ear canal, close to the cerebellum. We're contacting the oncohematological department of the children's hospital and the Ear, Nose and Throat Clinic immediately to arrange for the operation. The tumor must be removed as soon as possible."

We couldn't break the silence. Tears kept falling down my cheeks. Nail, as he was sharing our pain, kept sleeping calmly. We looked at our son mesmerized; we looked at each other with my husband, and then we stared out of the window that didn't even have a curtain. There were thousands of questions, unspoken charges and judgments roaming inside my head. I felt helpless. But all the sentences were divided by a full stop. It was just one single word. I heard the soft sound of the church bell. It became louder and louder.

It kept repeating one word. One short question. The same as we had.

WHY? WHY? WHY?

There was no answer.

People changed around us. They were empathetic. They brought us hot food, and no one reported us for being next to our son's bed all the time.

They didn't perform the surgery. We had another medical examination, an MRI scan, this time at the Diagnostic Center. The presence of the tumor was confirmed.

The next morning, a biopsy was performed in the OR of the clinic. We hoped that it was a benign tumor.

The head doctor of the department of infectious diseases asked what we would like to do.

We told him that we wanted our son to be transferred to the oncology department of the Children's' Clinic we contacted.

In the meantime, Nail's anemia became severe, and he needed a blood transfusion.

Our last weekend here was unforgettable. It was a sunshiny day of April. We were walking in the park of the hospital all day, close to the hundred years' old Turkish monuments.

Csingiz kept picking flowers and putting them into Nailka's hands; Nail was laughing with joy and threw the flowers into the air. By the time we had finished our walk, the backyard of the hospital had been covered with myriads of purple and yellow petals.

For a few hours, we seemed like a normal happy family.

I painted this picture on the last page of my virtual memory book when, after twenty days of hardships, we finally left.

Chapter 3

IN PARENTHESES

One month passed without me writing a single word.

I was unable to do so.

I had been thinking about the curative process over and over again.

After the hospital, our five-month stay at the clinic had finally ended. We had a lot of tests and, in most of the cases, I just closed my eyes and pretended that this wasn't happening to us. This was just a bad dream, and I was going to wake up soon.

I'm not going to write down everything we went through. I'll share fragments of our painful journey. Some of the stories are way too morbid to be credible… I still have a lot of stories to share.

Memories keep coming back from those times. I remember how frustrated, helpless, and "anti-hospital" I was.

Thousands of questions, thousands of feelings, thousands of moments of silence…

Today is the twentieth anniversary of that early morning when I had to take my seven-year-old son to hospital. The children's clinic was on duty. At the registration, they treated us reluctantly. They told that we had to wait because the internist would arrive around 8 o'clock. We still had a lot of time, and Csingiz's condition got worse. He was dehydrated and about to faint.

I was already used to fighting. I opened my mouth, and they called the doctor on duty. She was smiling and it felt good. She recognized us since we had met several times when we were here with Nailka.

I tried to tell her the clinical history with tears in my eyes and my voice trembling. I was talking about an excursion, a tick, the headaches, the vomiting and the avoidance of light.

Everything coincided. The signs were suggesting meningitis. Someone who went through hell knows that life is not an easy game. My son had become a shadow of himself in less than twelve hours.

Is this our fate?

We are in the same building where Nail was treated.

Csingiz got his treatment right away. Infusion. Blood test. They also performed a spinal test on him. This is a procedure in which a needle is inserted into the spinal canal to collect cerebrospinal fluid for diagnostic testing.

I thought I'd never get rid of the nightmares.

Csingiz had panic attacks. He was afraid of death. He was terrified of the thought of having a serious disease. When my husband saw him lying on the hospital bed with an infusion in his arm, he started crying and couldn't enter the room for half an hour.

I felt that panic was taking control over my body, and I was very close to losing someone I loved, my child. Suddenly everything vanished from my head. All the bad memories, pain, and humiliation. Nothing and nobody mattered but Csingiz.

Given the circumstances, they allowed me to stay for the night. I'm grateful for that.

Again, I couldn't sleep. I was standing by the window and watched the rain pouring outside. Everything was familiar: the trees, the lamp posts, the bumpy road.

Teardrops were rolling down my face. I stared into the stars, and I felt I should give up.

I was thinking of Nail. And God… I was praying for help and strength.

The next morning, Csingiz woke up cheerfully. He was a real hero when they performed additional blood tests and fundus examination. He looked happy and healthy again. Just like before.

Five days later, we were allowed to go home because the terrifying symptoms disappeared from one day to the next.

I know that Nail was there to help us that night. He showed us an evidence of eternity. He proved that spiritual contact does exist. All we can do is be thankful and appreciate who we are.

I freed myself from the hate and anger toward nurses and doctors. I wanted to see clearly.

That day I understood that the soul that had escaped from the cage of remission had returned to me from another dimension.

Could a greater miracle take place than for a mother to experience this?

Chapter 4
INTERLUDE

Nail would've been three years old on the 3rd of January 2002. I was still unable to convince myself to carry on with my book at that time. It felt like there was some kind of invisible power that prevented me from doing it.

One week later, I got a used computer and started writing. I worked mainly at night. I typed in around 240,000 characters in twenty days. I felt I was beyond the deadlock.

On the last Sunday of the month, the mirror in the hall just fell off the wall and broke into a million pieces. That is said to be a sign of misfortune.

Two days later, on the 29th of January, my computer crashed, and my files were lost forever. All I had left was a single title.

At that point, I thought I should give up. I don't believe in coincidence. But if I gave up, I wouldn't be worthy of my son. He has never doubted for a minute.

Once Jesus said to a pathfinder: "Never take no for an answer."

This was the clearest thought that accompanied me throughout our painful experience. I was challenged again and again. And I had to grow up to the task.

Chapter 5

HELL ON EARTH

We parked our car in the garden of the clinic.

We found a free spot at the back entrance, and we got out of the car. I was holding Nailka and a folder full of documents as we entered the corridor of oncology. Ruslan followed us carrying our stuff. It was noon. The long gloomy corridor was silent like it was the portal of a completely different world.

The doors opened. Children and their parents appeared at the doorways. Their faces looked pale, and the light had already faded from their eyes.

For a moment, I thought we were there by mistake. I turned Nailka around to spare him from the horrors of the situation. First, I wanted to run away, but then I halted. We had to stay. No one ever told us what lay ahead of us. Today I realized that it wouldn't be an easy ride but a tough and scary journey full of dangers.

The sad, tired eyes, bald heads only seem scary at first. It soon becomes clear that behind the exterior forced by circumstance lie real, beautiful souls.

The children roll mounts in front of them, a long tube leading from the bottle of colorful liquid on the top to under their pajamas. There are some who have no strength to walk, so they roll around in wheelchairs, but even they are able to shine a sudden smile that tells you they will never give up. They are brothers in this hell on Earth, and if needed they will be brothers in the heavens above.

The walls remember decades of painful screams, prayers of desperate parents calling for help, an eternal hope for their children's recovery. Since the world was born.

These vibrating tracks left here as mementos by victorious and defeated families then fuse together and give the glimmer of embers in the eyes of these little patients. Nobody is left behind by the guards of foregone memories, the shadow-silhouettes of hundreds and thousands of parents, relatives, and friends.

After fifteen minutes, a smiling nurse stepped up to us, took our documents, and led us to Ward 2. We were greeted by Winnie the Pooh's smile from the door's glass, the inseparable jar of honey in his hands.

I was pleasantly surprised by the roomy 3x5 meter ward's interior after my experience from the last few days. Yellow draperies with children's patterns separated the wards like a symbolic veil over outdated medical practices when personal freedom used to mean nothing.

Besides the two adult sized beds and the cot, there was a color TV and a kitchen table in the room. The old nightstands and chairs painted white are mementos of a long gone era. There was no mirror in the bathroom, just strip curtains blocking the view from the back garden. Quite eclectic, but at least they try to create a cozy atmosphere. Nevertheless, I felt I was in an orphanage from the last century. The government deports these sick children to a place that is anything but intimate and peaceful.

We met our doctors during the visit at noon. The professor was a well-known expert in the field; he was even awarded the title "Doctor of the Year" a few years earlier. It must be hard to cope with losing dozens of children, but it might give them enough strength to see some of these children recover.

There were two young dedicated but still uncertain doctors as well. And the nurses who were responsible for much more than they were qualified for. So, we met dedicated and less dedicated, empathetic and grumpy people here. Old and young as well.

I was thankful because the professor gave me permission to stay every night. I didn't have to sleep on a chair, and I didn't even have to pay for the bed. I used to be very sensitive those days, and nice gestures made me cry. I felt numb, but I could hear the professor's calm and soft voice.

"This is definitely a malignant tumor. Considering the CT and MRI scans, the blood test results, the anemia, the abnormally low number of platelets, the high number of leukocytes and LDH (serum level of lactate dehydrogenase), and the enlarged spleen and liver, I would say that this might be leukemia or lymphoma. We need to perform a bone marrow biopsy. He'll be given anesthesia."

"What does it mean?"

"We use a larger needle to withdraw a sample of solid bone marrow tissue. The biopsy needle is specially designed to collect a core of bone marrow. Subsequently, we analyze the sample. And since these symptoms must be signs of a more severe case, not just his ear, another medical intervention should be performed during the biopsy. Therefore, we won't just withdraw bone marrow, but with another needle, we'll inject a dose of chemotherapeutic agent into the cerebrospinal fluid."

"Is it really necessary?"

"Yes, it is. And we need to act fast. We're scheduling an appointment with the surgery. We need to perform the operation within one or two days so that we can start his therapy."

"Professor, do I understand correctly that my son has two types of tumors?"

"We don't know yet. When our colleagues detected the tumor, they suspected Rhabdomyosarcoma considering his young age and the location of the tumor, but we haven't received the biopsy results yet. We'll know more when they arrive. At this stage, we can't be sure that these two disorders are related. Personally, I would also take a third type of tumor, PNET (primitive neuroectodermal tumor), into consideration."

I couldn't believe it. This was incredible. I just sat there and couldn't say anything. My husband neither. We looked at each other, then at our son, and rocked him in silence. I started crying. My whole body was shaking. Nail stared at me with his blue eyes wide open, and I could see fright in those eyes. He had never seen us looking so desperate.

The next day brought further lab tests. They proved what we already knew. He was given antipyretic for his fever. He was pale and lethargic. He crouched down in his bed. He hadn't even pooped for days.

In the afternoon, I had to do some paperwork. They made me sign a lot of documents and informed consents.

On the 12th of April, I held my child and carried him at the entrance of the OR. I could feel my heart beat in my throat. I was extremely nervous.

"Please, take care of him," I told a man in green, but I wanted to scream instead.

The door closed behind them. A nice doctor called me to the nurses' station. Ruslan went out to the lobby to get some coffee, and probably he didn't want me to see him cry. He always wanted to stay strong. During our marriage, I saw him cry only once.

The nice doctor turned out to be an anesthesiologist, and she needed an extra signature for one of the documents. She smiled at me on her way back to the OR.

Before the operation, I asked one of the doctors about the expected length of the surgery.

"We should be ready in forty minutes," he replied.

I looked at my watch and started to count the minutes. The thrill was numbing. They said it's a routine surgery, but I was so worried about Nail.

I leaned against the wall next to the door as I was guarding the OR. I heard the children laughing in the nearby lounge area. I've never felt myself so lost and vulnerable.

"Maybe they are wrong, and it is not so serious. Please, God. Let it be so."

Time passed slowly. The last spark of youth died inside me as my shoulders began to bend forward, and new wrinkles appeared on my face every minute.

After two hours of waiting, the ground began to slip out from under my feet. Black dots started to dance before my eyes. I was scared. I wanted to hold him in my arms. I heard distorted voices from the distance. Everything went black, and I was about to collapse.

A touch on my shoulder brought me back to reality.

"Everything went fine. Look, there he is," the nice anesthesiologist told me, smiling.

And there he was. A young surgeon was holding him in his arms. He was still sleeping.

"What was taking so long?" I asked the anesthesiologist. "Was there any complication? I was told it wouldn't take longer than forty minutes."

"Oh, yes," she replied cheerfully. "You know, we have to prepare for the operation. We have to put on our surgical clothing, wash our hands and arms. It could take a lot of time. We're over it. This is what matters."

"You should've told me that it could be longer. I was scared to death. We love him so much."

I burst into tears and ran out to find my husband and tell him that the operation was over.

We were guarding his dream. At the time of the regular visit, we were told to leave the room. My husband was about to leave, but I decided to stay. What if Nail wakes up and can't see me? After all he's been through. My place is right here, next to him.

I must have been under the shock of the operation. The nurse asked me again to leave, but I insisted. And I won. She hurried away angrily.

As I was sitting alone in the silent room with glass walls, I had an uneasy feeling. Maybe I should've left.

I could see the other room through the glass. I could count around twenty doctors. They approached slowly. From bed to bed. They seemingly knew some the children, many of whom started to cry for their parents. I already regretted acting stubbornly. Nail was sleeping still.

I decided to leave the room before the visiting team entered, though I wanted to be back by the time Nail woke up. I slipped out of the room and hid behind an open door so that they wouldn't notice me. I was close enough to hear their conversation.

"Who is he?"

"Nail Haszjanov from oncology. He was transferred from the children's hospital. They considered his high fever a symptom of viral infection. He had been treated with antibiotics, but his condition hasn't improved. Then they suspected mononucleosis, and the otologist diagnosed him with myringitis bullosa. During the next control, they detected lesions in the right middle ear. They performed CT and MRI scans. He arrived the day before yesterday. We're waiting for his biopsy results. His other test results and his enlarged liver and spleen suggest that the blast cells are present in other tissues as well. Today we performed bone marrow biopsy and also injected a dose of chemotherapeutic agent into the cerebrospinal fluid."

"Why did it take so long to bring him here?" asked one of the professors angrily. "It wouldn't be the first time to have a patient who should've been taken here much earlier. We really should clarify a few things…" And he didn't finish the sentence as our eyes met.

There was no need to ask who I was. He could see it clearly from my face. I ran along the corridor. I'd heard enough.

Nail was still sleeping when I returned. I was thankful he waited for us.

When he woke up, he was irritable and had a hoarse voice. His cheeks were flaming, and he was gasping for breath. I ran out to the nurses' station for help, but they said that these are normal reactions after anesthesia. He had been monitored for two more hours and – after twenty hours of starvation and because he didn't throw up – he was allowed to drink some water and eat some food.

He was moved back to his room for the night. I couldn't sleep, and I wanted to find out why. As I was searching through my virtual memory book, I found a picture from a dream. It happened before Nail got sick.

I heard a soft voice. I was in a chapel, and two figures were standing in front of me: one of them appeared to be a teacher. The other one was his assistant. I couldn't remember the face of the latter. The other one was a shape shifter. I knew it because when he looked at me, I asked: "Who are you?"

"Anyone you want me to be…" he replied.

Then he transformed himself into someone else multiple times. When he decided to stop, he was wearing a long brown habit of a monk. His voice was sharp, but it didn't scare me. Now he looked somewhat familiar. That's it! He was my long forgotten teacher. I could barely remember him, like he was coming back from my thousand years' old memory. He was not bothered by my confused mind at all. He seemed to treat my condition as normal. He was talking to me, but I couldn't remember his words. In that moment, I realized why I was there with them. I felt I belonged with them. Then I started falling, and I saw them leave through a door. I shouted: "No! Don't go away! Stay with me!"

But they wouldn't listen. I felt something special. Something like fresh air. I was calm and happy, and I didn't want this to end.

I felt Nail's hand on my face as I woke up. I was disappointed to wake up for another day leaving my mysterious visitors behind. I was longing for them, for that tingling feeling. But no matter how hard I tried, I could never go back to that peaceful place.

I felt lonely. I knew that I was left alone in this world. No one ever would understand how important my child is for me. And I knew that they wouldn't do everything for my child to recover.

I couldn't decide whether I wanted the night to end or not. There was another operation scheduled for Nail in the morning.

It was an emergency case. He got a central venous catheter (CVC) placed in his chest. They usually remain in place for a longer period than other venous access devices, especially when the reason for their use is long-standing. Central line insertions may cause several complications. Of course, I had to sign some papers again. I felt vulnerable and thought it's unfair to pass responsibility on to others. I hate this in everyday life as well.

Nail was in good hands that day. The operation went very fast and without complications. He got a plastic device implanted in his artery under his right collarbone. A straw sized line was hanging out of his chest 6-8 centimeters down under the stitches. It could be used for infusions or could be closed when there was no need to use it.

Sterile technique is highly important when living with CVC, as a line may serve as an entry point for pathogenic organisms. Additionally, the line itself may become infected with bacteria. The doctor put it this way: if we touch the line without proper sterilization and disinfection, it is like we are touching a human heart with bare hands.

We waited in the surgery for Nailka to wake up. We were asked to take the child down to X-ray because they wanted to make sure everything was in place. There were not enough nurses to accompany us.

We needed to grow into our roles. I was holding my son, and my husband was following us with an infusion bottle in his hand. We moved slowly. Finally, we found the X-ray department on the ground floor.

Blood was running back from the cannula inside the line that was hanging out from his chest. We started panicking. We didn't know what to do. Of course, all we had to do is to raise the bottle, but we were not informed. First, we thought it was coming out from the wound, and we started shouting at each other. Nail woke up crying. It was a helpless feeling that we could cause him pain. He only calmed down when we arrived back in the room.

I couldn't sleep that night. I placed the little chair next to Nail's cot and held his hand. I was afraid that he might pull out the cannula. I'd been told during the visit that it was very important not to let him touch it. Unfortunately, it's not easy to tell these rules to a fifteen-month-old child. Though, I didn't want to bind his little hands. Just like most of the parents, I became a volunteer nurse in a few days.

By Friday, the test results of the biopsy, the bone marrow, and the cerebrospinal fluid were partially ready. Acute leukemia and lymphoma in the bone marrow were verified. We were still waiting for the analysis of the tissue samples from the tumor.

On that day – the 14th of April 2000 – Nailka's treatment was started following the regulations of the international INTERFANT-98 protocol.[1]

In the first, so-called induction phase of the therapy, the doctors try to eliminate as many cancer cells as possible. The aim is to lower their number under 5% in the blood and bone marrow. If we succeed, we can continue with the next phase, called remission phase.[2]

The tumor in Nail's right ear caused venous circulatory disorder as well; therefore, the doctors decided to treat him with daily doses of Fraxiparine to prevent thrombosis. The place where they inserted the needle inflamed, so they were switching between his arms and thighs.

Nail's condition got worse. His ear began to ache, and he had a high fever again. He was lethargic, just lying in my arms or in his bed all day. After nine days, his blood test results required another blood transfusion.[3]

---

1. Increasing doses of Prednisolone oral tablet. It's a hormone, not an antineoplastic agent. In terms of mechanism of action, it causes metabolic disorders so that cell division and multiplication are blocked.
2. It means that the signs and symptoms of cancer are reduced. The expression comes from the Latin remissio meaning "to suppress." This phase is very important in the path toward recovery. Although it doesn't mean someone in this phase is fully recovered. It involves long months of maintenance therapy, and after five years – if cancer cells don't come back – the patient has recovered from the illness.

I started reading and collecting books about alternative methods in cancer care. I got obsessed with those treatments. I believed that if we tried hard enough, I'd find a solution and we'd succeed.

I knew that the doctors in the clinic would refuse these alternative methods. They only believed in Western medicine, in surgical removal, in chemo- and radiotherapy. In our case, surgical removal of the tumor couldn't be considered since cancer cells were already present everywhere in his body. Radiotherapy was not used in children under three, particularly not in their brain.

So, we had one choice left. Chemotherapy.

Chemotherapy is not selective, meaning it kills healthy cells along with the cancer cells. This inflicts serious damage on the body. Chemotherapy agents suppress the bone marrow by damaging the blood-producing cells, and my son was about to face serious side effects.

The alternative methods are not so drastic, although I had to narrow down the choices given my son's very young age. I concentrated on principles and methods that might be useful in our case. I thought that if I managed to merge alternative methods with Western medicine, Nail would recover. I still believe that is true.

I was only reading about the theory of such methods, but there was nobody from whom I could learn the practices. And I had no idea where to start. Natural medicine has its own rules. I believed that God would show me the way.

I spent hours making phone calls. There were fewer and fewer names on my list. Some of them were unreachable; others didn't even want to come near the hospital. I'd had enough of it. I was aware of the pros and cons of both approaches. But the life of my son was in danger. I would've done anything for him. Therefore, I needed every support from both sides.

Obviously, it meant that I was between two fires. The Western treatments are local, only considering the cancer itself. Chemotherapy is fast, and it

---

3. Decrease in the number of platelets, red and white blood cells in the blood can be very dangerous. If left untreated, it can progress and cause bone marrow failure. This is why it is necessary to have regular blood tests. If there's a decrease in protein numbers, the immune system can't protect the body, and it can cause high fever, fungal, or bacterial infection. Doctors usually treat it with antibiotics. A low hemoglobin level is referred to as anemia or low red blood count. In case of external or internal bleeding, it would be hard to stop the bleeding. One of the symptoms of anemia is that cells can't carry enough oxygen. This condition may require intervention in the form of blood transfusion.

stops the growth of cancer cells. Natural medicine is holistic. It considers all aspects of life: physical, psychological, social, and spiritual. It helps the body to heal itself and can be more effective than non-holistic Western treatments. And it takes time.

In case of Nail, time was the key word. The types of cancers that occur most often in children are different from those seen in adults. Several types of cancer are virtually unique to children, but the cancers most often seen in adults – including those of the lung, breast, and stomach – are extremely rare in children. Cancer in children is also more malignant since their cells are younger and multiply rapidly. But it also implies that these cells are more vulnerable; therefore, they respond well to treatments. Combined with natural medicine, the survival rates are significantly higher.

I decided to choose this path.

I knew that I had nothing to lose. I saw in the doctors' eyes that Nail was giving up. They didn't say it though. They were just talking about numbers, percentages, and possibilities between 30% and 95%. They never denied the complex nature of my son's disease. Moreover, they said Nail's case was unique. They'd never seen something like this before. But I could feel their uncertainty. They were just groping about in the dark. I still believed that my son was in good hands. The only thing I was missing was honesty. I might have made different choices.

After having read tons of books, I was still looking for the most suitable method of treatment. These books were mainly about cancer in adults. One day a saleswoman of a bookstore gave me a name with a number. I made the call the same day. First I could just speak with a nice lady, but later the naturopath called me back.

I told him everything about our journey so far, and this was the first time I felt that someone was listening to me. He didn't interrupt me, and he didn't think I was crazy. He was just listening to me.

"This is incredible," he said when I finished my monologue.

I asked him for help. I told him that I wouldn't be able to go through with it alone. I needed someone who could help me when I got stuck.

First he was not sure about this, and I didn't know why. I told him that Nail was in bad shape, and it was impossible to bring him home. I asked him, I begged him not to let me down just because Nail was in hospital. I told him to forget about his prejudices and help us.

On the weekend, Laci and Gyöngyi, the two naturopaths, visited us in the hospital.

They were shocked by the grim atmosphere of the hospital. When Nail fell asleep, I left my son to Ruslan, and I went out to the garden with the couple. The sun was shining, and I realized the contrast between the hospital room and the garden. My eyes hurt; the vibrant colors were dancing in front of me, and I felt dizzy. I hated the liveliness of all of this. I burst into tears, and these two people just sat there holding my hands softly.

I pulled myself together and thanked them for coming. Laci said that there seems to be no future in it. Nailka is dying.

I was Nail's only hope. How could I give up the fight?

I accompanied Laci and Gyöngyi back to their car. I asked how much I had to pay for this consultation. They were almost offended by my question. They said they always listen to their heart, and they wouldn't accept any money. It was their mission.

The same day, on the 20th of April, we had the first chemotherapy.[4]

Nail tolerated the treatment quite well. His appetite and mood improved. The doctors attributed all of these to the hormone injection, but I knew that there was something else in the background. My son completely transformed within a few hours. He could sit again and even tried to stand up in his cot holding the side of the bed. The professor noticed Nailka's improvement as well.

The next day, they performed another bone marrow biopsy and also injected a dose of methotrexate into the cerebrospinal fluid.

---

[4]. The medical records looked like this:
  Inj. Zofran 3X2 mg (emetics)
  Inj. Claforan 3X500 mg (antibiotics)
  VCR (Vincristin) 0.75 mg to the bolus (cytostatics)
  Inj. Amikin 3X50 mg (antibiotics)
  DRB (Daunorubicin) 15 mg, 100 ml diluted in R-5 (cytostatics)
  Tabl. Milurit 3X0.5
  Sol. Leavovit 1X1 drop (Vitamin D)
  Sol. Contramal 3X4 drops (painkiller)
  Ara-C 37.5 mg, 50 ml diluted in R-5 (cytostatics)
  Inj. Oradexon 2X1.5 mg (hormone, ten times stronger than Prednisolon)
  Inj. Fraxiparine 0.2 ml (antithrombotics)
  Sol. Paxirasol 3X2 ml (for his cough, added to the list after the daily visit)

Diagnostic developments were not reported. Though I was happy to see that the tumor behind his ear almost completely disappeared, and the liver and spleen enlargement had also improved. After five weeks of intensive treatment in the hospital, Nailka's fever declined.

The progress surprised the doctors as well. From this point, I think they started to believe in Nail's recovery.

We could continue Nail's treatment according to the protocol, without any delay.

On the 27th of April, the fifth time that month, we were standing in front of the OR again, waiting for an operation that aimed to introduce cytostatic into the central nervous system. Of course, we were worried. Our child was to be considered an urgent case. Nevertheless, we had to wait until the afternoon for the operation. This means that he was not allowed to eat or drink for half a day. Again, they said it was urgent. Really? What could've been more urgent than a child with cancer? He should've been the first to be operated on in the morning. Nailka was crying in my arms full of pain, and I felt helpless.

I had no problems with the surgery except for this. It felt good to be among those smiley and positive people, for that matter.

On the last Thursday before Easter, I left the hospital a few times. Ruslan spent the whole night with Nail.

There were five people sitting in the car, including me. We were heading to a holy place of pilgrimage. We were going to have a mass celebrated for the recovery of my son. The church was dedicated to the Virgin Mary. I loved this place. The calming, tranquil atmosphere. The silence. The intimacy.

I didn't like the mass, but the beauty of the church really touched me. I looked at the frescos of the Virgin Mary and the angels, and all I could think of was my child. I regretted not staying with him in the hospital. I missed him a lot.

I prayed to the Virgin Mary to take care of my child and not betray us no matter what happened in the next months.

At home I took a long warm bath. Csingiz was happy to see me, and we chatted a lot. It helped clear my head.

Before going to bed, I reached for my phone. Nail was already sleeping, and Ruslan's voice sounded calm. I thought it was time to make the step I'd been planning for so long.

I had a pen pal. We got to know each other from a newspaper ad back in 1994 when Csingiz was born. We had been writing to each other ever since. For special events, Antonella always surprised Csingiz – and later Nail – with something nice. She has become my best friend. My soul mate. I've told her my best-kept secrets, and I knew that our friendship lacked the poison of self-interest. We had each other's phone numbers, but we kept the illusion and contacted each other only via letters. Lella, that was her nickname, was an Italian lady from Bormio. She had two sons just like me. Francesco, as old as Csingiz, and Alessandro, as old as Nail. We were planning to meet that summer to spend a few days together. But I knew that it wouldn't happen. And Lella didn't expect anything.

I dialed the number and, in the next moment, I heard her surprised voice. Her mood changed when I said, "Nail has cancer." Then I started to cry and couldn't say anything... Lella was terrified. She was the best mother I've ever known. She was always patient and loving, and family was the most important thing for her. Now there was a woman hundreds of kilometers away who could fully sympathize with my sorrow. I was inexpressibly thankful. She gave me a lot of strength.

The next day, the hospital was like a disturbed ant hill. It was Friday, and everybody was packing to leave for the Easter holiday.

I prepared the Easter nest on our little table in the room, and we were waiting for Dad and brother to celebrate like a normal family.

There was just a little Arabian girl, Amani, and us in the department. All of the other patients were sent home. Her Yemeni mother was guarding Amani, and her father (also from Yemen, working in Hungary as a doctor) was at work. Amani was a beautiful little girl with huge brown eyes and creole skin. Just like a princess. And when I looked at Nail and Amani, I knew that cancer doesn't select according to nationality, religion, or wealth. For me, Nail was my own jewel from within, and Amani symbolized the wide-open world. As for now, Amani is gone.

I kept wondering about establishing a foundation to help these families. I knew exactly what the parents needed and when and how they needed it.

First of all, the parents needed a lawyer to secure the balance of power between them and the medical staff. A lawyer who is able to represent them. A lawyer who is aware of the current legislations and patients' rights. On the other hand, a good lawyer could recommend appropriate healthcare services, as well as governmental and non-governmental financial support. I didn't know anything about these opportunities, and I didn't have enough time or strength to ask the medical staff about such things at that time.

Another important step would be to search for child-friendly psychiatrists. Their task would be to help the families process everything they were going through, including the loss of other children.

We would need to create a network of hospice houses and dedicated hospice teams, which could develop care plans that met each patient's individual need for pain management and symptom control. We are not taught how to treat a dying child or how to mourn or how to behave with someone who has lost their loved one. These are taboos, and someone should break this crazy cycle.

For children with cancer, maintaining a healthy diet is also of great importance. Proper nutrition is a vital tool in the fight against cancer, so my foundation would employ a nutritionist to help these families.

And if I had enough power and influence, I would fight to raise the minimum wage of those working in the medical sector as well as solving their everyday problems and hardships.

Sweeping our problems under the carpet won't be helpful. Therefore, we need to establish acceptable working conditions –with the financial help of the foundation – in healthcare facilities. Because we need to respect these people trying their best to save lives.

The holidays passed slowly, and we were counting the days before we could go home.

During the first week of May, Nail got his doses of cytostatics every day; these are cancer drugs that inhibit cell growth and division. His blood test results looked quite disturbing again. Red cells and platelets were introduced into his system to prevent bone marrow failure. On the 4th of May, he had another operation during which they injected drugs into the cerebrospinal fluid. On this day, he got another chemotherapy drug, an agent called L-asparaginase, for the third time. It had a specific side effect: allergy.

Nail hadn't produced any allergic symptoms. His values like his weight and height were measured weekly so that the doctors could determine the exact dose of the agents.[5]

The next afternoon, on Friday, the detailed test results of the bone marrow and the tumor arrived.[6]

Our doctors decided to continue the current protocol, the Infant 98 therapy.

The 4th of May. The date I'll never forget.

On Friday afternoon, the doctor said that we were allowed to go home for a short time. I was surprised, but at the same time, I was happy for the two days that we were going to spend together at home. The doctor must have noticed my happy tears as I started packing because she closed the door behind her smiling.

We could go home for the first time in six weeks.

It was like all of us had been reborn at that moment. The four of us just stood there at the entrance – Ruslan and Csingiz hurried out hearing me shut the taxi door – and for a short moment, we believed in the miracle… That it was over, it had passed, it was only a mistake.

The sun was shining down on us from the clear sky above, and the world was busy. People were arguing over everyday nothings, running around doing their errands, and by the time we came to, we were shut out from this strange noisy and busy Ferris wheel. Time slowed, and then stopped altogether. We were looking at ourselves from outside as we slowly and ceremoniously walked through every room watching Nail's eyes as he recognized that he came back to us. I didn't know which the bigger illusion was: believing that all of us were dreaming the same thing, or dreaming that all of us were awake.

But nobody wanted to answer.

---

5. Intravenous fluid must be given at a specific rate, neither too fast nor too slow. The specific rate may be measured as ml/hour, L/hour, or drops/min. To control or adjust the flow rate, only drops per minute are used. If the fluid is infused too quickly, it can cause high fever, nausea, and vomiting. If it is too slow – especially in case of blood fluids – the device can become blocked by clotted blood.
6. According to the results, there was a massive immature – so called CD33, CD34 co – tumor in the bone marrow and a small-cell, partially polymorph CD34-MIC2-Synaptophysin carcinoma in Nail's ear. It also read as follows: "The nature and the histogenesis of the process can't be determined. We had a concilium where we concluded that on morphological basis and despite the unusual immunophenotype, the immature mielomonocytaer nature of the tumor is unlikely. Based on the tests on bone marrow and the tissue sample from the ear, IgH and TCR gamma-monoclonal gene rearrangements are not present which also excludes the possibility of a limphoreticular process. Overall, in order to provide a more accurate histogenesis, we would need additional genetic tests."

Nail filled the house with life, and we let him enchant us behind his magical screen, and the whole house was humming with the rhythm of the ode of a real heart, like a lit vein through a wrist, pumping the blood bond of eternal connection.

That evening there was a Mother's Day celebration in the kindergarten. At that moment, nobody knew better than me what it meant to be a mother and to fight for the status to remain one.

That Friday night was one of my most favorite Mother's Days. At home the four of us could finally get under the safe, warm blankets and dream of a better tomorrow like refugees running from reality.

On Sunday, we returned to the clinic where the chemotherapy resumed. The side effects of the treatment could already be felt: Nail often had a fever, he vomited and had metabolic disorders, but his hair didn't fall out. We tried to use all natural methods to soften the blows from the side effects and support a rapid regeneration of his body.

I watched with wide eyes every time Laci massaged Nail's sole and other body parts or gave him energetic treatment. He encouraged me to do these exercises regularly as often as I could, especially on zones that, according to the sciences of reflexology, activate blood-forming organs. Every night after he went to sleep, I massaged Nail over with careful motions from the knee down with special attention to his ankle bones, the area around his Achilles tendon, and the whole of his sole.

Sometimes I lost myself in the activity. I was doing it with such love and faith that I didn't notice that it was past midnight and dawn was starting outside in the faraway lands of healthy people and children. I became a prisoner in a state that not only took my physical sense of time but also destroyed my presuppositions about the real world. I was drifting toward an irrational barrier because I knew I could only hope to find the catharsis I desired there.

In nutrition, I followed the main principles of macrobiotics. We mostly gave Nail cereals, green vegetables, bio-bread and fresh fruit. A man can sustain this kind of diet for years if he pays careful attention to avoid deficiency diseases. Brown rice, boiled potatoes with a little olive oil and spice mix formed the basis of the diet, together with beetroot and carrot juice. I varied this menu by adding boiled millet, rye, barley, buckwheat, wheat or bulgur. To prevent osteoporosis, I added tahini or sesame salt, both of which contain great amounts of calcium. All of these can be obtained in bio shops and most hypermarkets, which are larger than supermarkets and sell clothes, electronic devices, and other products aside from food. Sometimes, I made meals from nuts as they not only make the bowels move but are also beneficial to the heart. Almond milk too is very nutritious and contains a lot of calcium.

Everybody who knew about this told us not to tell the doctors because they would become worried that the child might choke on one of the small seeds. But using this logic, they could choke on anything. Of course, we never left Nail alone, and we were careful not to stress his body too much with such food. Nevertheless, he needed the calories.

I gave him the leguminous plants mixed together with added ground cumin to avoid distension. He regularly got vegetable dishes made from lentil, peas, or beans. From dairy products, I mostly favored natural yogurts that contained living culture. I added sesame salt, tahini, and oat bran when he had digestive problems. If I judged that he lost weight, I gave him chestnut paste but sometimes also ground poppy seeds, pumpkin seeds, and sunflower seeds.

His diet got revitalized by summertime vegetables and fruits.

He never even once received sweetened drinks or ones containing artificial coloring, instant cocoa or coffee products. We threw out all preserved, salted, conserved food. The bio juices, herbal teas, and decarbonized mineral water proved to be perfect for quenching his thirst. As a self-appointed researcher and dietetic, I discovered "rice milk" that was made from brown rice in the local supermarket. I still regard it as a sensational product.

On the 15th of May, according to protocol, Nail received his sixth L-asparaginase treatment. The morning nurse was quite hasty because she wanted to hand over the department with all the treatments done so as to avoid her colleagues' annoyance for leaving behind so much work. Here and there, she made the IV drip faster. To be honest, I didn't really pay attention to what she was doing because she was constantly talking to me. She told me that we were out of time, so she had to up the drip count. We got the treatment, they shut Nail's central canola, and we started off home to enjoy our one and a half days off.

Even in the cab, I had a bad feeling. Nail started getting red, and his face was heating up. I asked the taxi driver to roll the windows down. Maybe he was only hot. I was looking forward to getting home and spending a few hours together, just the four of us. Nail had fevers before from cytostatica, so I wasn't scared because I knew how to make it go away if needed. By the end of the ten minute long drive, Nail was coughing and retching, so I didn't feel so confident any more. It was around 4 p.m., and I knew that around this time there are no oncologists on the department, only the doctor on duty who oversees the different departments. I didn't want to go back and pass up our day off, yet I also felt that there was too much responsibility for me to make this decision alone. I took Nail into my room and took his clothes off. His temperature was almost 103 F. I noticed patches of red on his whole body, and both his knees turned red as if something had rubbed them. I wasn't sure if that was caused by the acceleration of the treatment, so I called our family doctor in her office on the other end of town. I told her everything and asked her to come and have a look at Nail.

She asked a few additional questions about Nail, mostly about his blood pressure, but we had no way to measure it. The doctor told us to urgently go back to the hospital because this condition could quickly become life-threatening, and she was too far away to be here on time. I immediately called Laci, the naturopath, to cry to him and tell him what had happened. He furiously cursed the family tree of the nurse who had been in a hurry and tried to calm me down. He too agreed with the doctor to get to the hospital as soon as possible, but meanwhile, she supplied me with useful tips. I sent Ruslan away to get Calli tea, which is probably the most well-known cleansing tea, only very expensive. Meanwhile, I pushed a few spoonfuls of boiled buckwheat through a filter and poured the thick paste into Nail's bottle, thinning it with some water. I let him drink it so as to purge the allergy causing toxins from his body as soon as possible. I called a taxi, but before it arrived, my husband had come back with a friend and the Calli tea. Tibi admitted that we needed to get to the doctor now, so before the taxi even arrived, he gave us a lift to the clinic. As was our usual misfortune, the doctor on duty had not practiced on the oncology department before. I saw that he didn't quite believe me because he found not much wrong with Nail, whose fever had already subsided after I gave him a suppository. He said it couldn't be an overdose or poisoning, so he probably only had a heat rash. I wanted to shake him, shout with him, make him understand that it was not the least in my interest to spend the night here again instead of home. I only asked him to put Nail on an IV drop to wash the toxins from his body. By that time, two nurses were trying to convince the doctor that it was the right call, or even to give him DIFA, a steroid, which is a good antidote. The doctor disappeared, as I later came to know, to study a medical encyclopedia, which is honorable, but I really wanted something to happen. I can understand if in such situations a doctor wants to weigh many different options, but I can't understand why she can't call for the help of her boss or an experienced professional. What shame is there in asking for help?

At last, after twenty long minutes, she came back, administered the DIFA, and opened the central canola. I was relieved, and right as she left, I started to actively detoxify Nail. I boiled, cooled, then sip by sip, I gave him lots of Calli tea. I prepared and gave him a chamomile enema. It was already late night when I finally felt we were past the worst part. Not only did we prevent a more serious problem with the DIFA, but we managed to detoxify a lot of toxins from his body.

I thought this would serve a good cautionary tale, but I was wrong…

The next such screw-up three weeks later almost cost me my son's life.

On May 18th at 6:30 a.m., we went into the diagnostics center for an MRI. We were really anxious to see whether the tumor had gotten smaller due to the cytostatics in his central nervous system.

As we went up and down, we did so with closed, sealed envelopes, so we could only count on the information given directly to us. According to that, the tumor did not get worse, but also didn't get better. At least it didn't cause venal circulation disorder, so we could leave off the painful injections aimed at preventing a thrombosis.[7] I looked at this as a small step forward.

Since our unplanned return on Monday, Nail was constantly and visibly feverish, weak, and without appetite. They put him on antibiotics and performed various tests to look for infections. The result was that they

---

7. Fraxiparine injection

found a fungal infection in the central canola (for the second time in ten days) that required the application of intravenous antifungal serum.

His fever went down in a few days, so on May 22nd, we could start the next phase of the Interfant 98 protocol.[8]

The next day, they did this treatment together with the bone marrow examination. They injected it into the cerebrospinal fluid during anesthesia. He endured the treatment for the next few days, but by then, even the injection[9] that was meant to prevent damage to his mucous membranes could not hold the side effects at bay. His penis got inflamed to such a degree that they immediately halted the cytostatic treatments and called for a surgeon to treat the damaged, sometimes bleeding, areas. Nail's blood tests got significantly worse, so they gave him blood and set him on an antibiotics treatment[10] twice a day. He had to take these continuously, every day, independently from the intravenous antibiotics treatments.

The inflammation of his penis did not want to go away. The side effects of medicines can be felt for weeks after treatment, so I started to worry. I called Laci, who was really angry about these serums and also a little with me for letting them do this to Nail. He told me to think about what this damaging liquid could have done inside his body if it could damage his penis to such an extent.

These days I started using aromatherapy during my massages. We had an assortment of essential oils hidden deep in our nightstand.

I took a deep breath and put together a mixture of oils. I chose olive and chestnut oil as carriers. I poured the base into a small dark bottle and added a few drops of chamomile, milfoil, and lavender oils that are known for their anti-inflammatory attributes. I mixed them together and then put a few drops on his diaper to see whether it bothered him. Nail didn't make a sound. An hour later, I became braver and applied it to his penis, and next time I poured it on the affected skin surface. Meanwhile, Laci and Gyöngyi arrived and, as I requested, they brought a bottle of tutsan oil that they had made. I awoke every hour during the night and alternatingly used either the tutsan oil or chamomile oil on the affected body parts. By

---

8. Application of the "MARAM cycle" HD (High dose) – Methotrexat block. This is an antimetabolite that is almost identical to the ones produced by the body. The body can't distinguish between the two so they attach to the DNA, disrupting cell reproduction. Especially in higher doses the Methotrexat causes a nasty and dangerous side effect – the inflammation of the mucous membranes.
9. Leukovorin-injection
10. Sumetrolim

morning, the results were so apparent, they even surprised me. The swelling and inflammation went away completely and the hot-red skin started to get back to normal. There was an unexpected side effect: chamomile oil has a dark blue color, so even though I applied it heavily diluted, it still managed to color Nail's penis blue. During visitation, I saw the puzzled look on the professor's face, but all in all, he too was relieved by the disappearance of the nasty inflammation.

At the beginning of June, we got the results of the bone marrow tests that showed that the remission was not complete: among the regenerating marrow colonies, there were still cancerous cell formations detectable. This meant only partial progress. According to the results in June, there was still no final diagnosis, and they also couldn't make additional statements about the tumor in his ear. For the time, they treated it as acute undifferentiated cellular leukemia (maybe MO a.k.a. acute myeloid leukemia).[11]

In the last few days, Nail started to reach for his ear more and more. We noticed this with Ruslan and immediately told our doctors that the area behind his ear had become frighteningly bigger. We did not see him experience big amounts of pain, so we didn't need painkillers, but to be sure, he was visited by an otologist for a few days. One of these visits was done not by our usual doctor but a colleague of his. He had crude, repulsing manners; at least that's what I felt during those few minutes we had to spend together. I asked him not to be rude with the child and to please tell me what he was seeing. He snapped back that he didn't understand that I couldn't see that his colleagues failed to catch the tumor with chemotherapy, so our chances didn't look good.

I started to feel more and more that we were left alone with our belief that Nailka could be cured.

In early June, they drew lots of blood from the whole family – all four of us to check whether one of us was compatible as a bone marrow donor if we needed to do a transplant.[12]

---

11. Diagnosis: AUL? AML-MO, metastasis pNET?
12. This is the so called HLA (Human Leukocyte Antigen) typization. HLA is a gene complex encoding the major histocompatibility complex (MHC) proteins in humans. These cell-surface proteins are responsible for the regulation of the immune system in humans. They are important in disease defense. They are the major cause of organ transplant rejections. HLA is found in most cells in our body. Our immune system uses HLA markers to know which cells belong in our body and which do not. Half of our HLA markers are inherited from our mother and half from our father. About 70% of three patients who need a transplant do not have a suitable donor in their family. In this case the transplant team may look for an unrelated donor.

Since Nail was still not in the remission phase, he was reclassified into a higher risk group, and the doctors started to talk about the possibility of bone marrow transplant. Stem cell implant was not an option because Nail's own bone marrow was affected by the disease. This is why they needed to check whether we were suitable donors or not. Five test tubes of blood were collected from all four of us.

Considering his young age and the frequent transfusions, it was outrageous that they needed this large quantity of blood from Nailka as well.

But the worst part of it was that two week later, when I asked the doctor about the results, she just said that our blood samples might have been lost because the results should've arrived by that time. I still don't know whether Csingiz, Ruslan, or I would've been suitable donors for Nailka.

During the short break in his treatment, Nail's blood test results normalized, his condition stabilized, and in order to make chemotherapy more efficient, the doctors decided to switch to another protocol.[13]

The first five days passed without any complications.

On 11th June, Nail got several treatments.[14] Most of them were almost over by noon. Before the last treatment, an unsettling feeling came to me. I was thinking of Nail's allergic reaction three week ago. I was afraid that it might happen again, and none of our usual doctors were on duty that day.

The young doctor adjusted the valve on the infusion to make the dripping a little slower. I saw that he wanted to calm me down, but I was extremely nervous. This time they used a different type of set called macro drip that delivers four times bigger drops than the usual one. Until now, everything went fine. The doctor returned and asked me to measure Nail's temperature frequently and be very alert for any suspicious signs. The fluid kept dripping, and everything looked fine. We ate our meal and played a bit. My mother-in-law was puttering around, and my husband went into the city.

I looked at the infusion bottle. Something was wrong. I'd never seen like this before, but the other parents warned me about such cases. There was no fluid in the tube. I jumped up, grabbed the tube, and started to find the end of the air bubble. I could feel my heart beat in my throat. I ripped

---

13. This time they chose the 6-day block of BFM-ALL-95 FRG HR-2 protocol.
14. He was given antibiotics (Fortum, Amikacin), fungicide (mycosyst) and two types of cytostatics (VBL and L-asparaginase).

Nail's shirt off, and just a few centimeters away from the cannula, I spotted the end of the fluid. I knew that if the air bubble entered my son's vein, it could cause an embolism and he might die. I needed to close the infusion set. The other parents taught me how to do it, but my hands were shaking. We didn't have enough time to call someone from the other end of the corridor. I needed to act. First, I turned the valve the wrong way and the bubble began to move faster. I panicked.

Oh, God. I'm killing my child, I thought, and I almost fainted. It was insane. I quickly pulled myself together and turned the valve the other way around. The bubble stopped one centimeter away from the cannula. At that moment, I felt like I was around 100 years old. I put my son into my mother-in-law's arms, and I ran out to the corridor to call for help.

"That was quite a big bubble," the young doctor said.

I watched him releasing the air from the tube, and his calmness tranquilized me as well. I held my son in my hands, and I put my arms around him. But this was just the beginning of our "horror show."

The fluid was dripping again. The nurse came in. She was fluttering nervously and was complaining about her co-workers. I barely listened. I just wanted to concentrate on my son. I thought that if I held him tight, I could save him from the cruel world. The nurse grabbed a little chair, placed it under the infusion set and stepped on it. She was too short; therefore, she needed something so that she could examine the infusion set.

"Oh, so this is why!" she shouted. "That stupid doctor forgot to open this thing. She thinks too much of herself. I'm opening the valve. We're late."

The whole thing happened in a second. When I raised my head, she had already left the room.

In the same minute, my son cried out in pain and touched his little hands. I looked at him, and there was a red spot on the back of his hand. It appeared from nowhere. And there was another. And another… Both of his hands were full of red spots.

"Oh, my God! What the hell is this?"

I looked at the macro drop set, and I saw that the valve was open. The poison was dripping into my son's body on full speed.

I closed the valve in a hurry, put Nail into the hands of my wailing mother-in-law and ran out for help. By this time Nail's neck and face were also full of red spots.

I found the grumpy nurse in the kitchen and asked her to help my son. We ran back to the room. She pulled out the infusion and took it to the operation room on the other side of the corridor. She wanted to hide the *corpus delicti*.

In the meantime, Nail went through a shocking transformation. It was like we were in a horror movie. His nose, ears, mouth, arms and legs swelled. I could barely see his eyes. In a matter of minutes, my beautiful son transformed into a swollen creature. My mother-in-law got sick and had to leave the room.

Another nurse rushed into the room as we were still shouting. She knew what to do. She grabbed the phone and rushed out heading toward the other building to find the doctor on duty.

By the time help arrived, the main character of the event – the morning nurse – returned, and quickly ran off to get the emergency tray with a puzzled look on her face.

Nail got lots of medicine through his cannula.[15]

All the doctors – including the adjunct on duty – surrounded us and observed. Everyone stood in silence. It was only broken by the voice of the morning nurse, who said she had to hurry to catch her bus home. After that nothing could be heard in the room but my "Don't worry, baby. It'll go away soon. You'll see." monologue as I stroked Nail's head trying to calm him. I read somewhere that in most emergency situations, people tend to die more from panic than from their actual problems. I wanted Nail to understand and believe that everything was under control, and he didn't need to be afraid. I was almost humming it to him like it was just the two of us, and I didn't for a moment stop stroking him. I think that at that moment, a sober madman took over my body and controlled my actions. My head heavy, feeling dizzy, I asked the doctor on duty with an idiotic smile in the corner of my mouth: "Doctor, will it pass? Tell me this thing will pass."

"We hope so. That's why we're still here," she replied silently.

---

15. He got Salsol, steroids (DIFA), Tonogen, and Calcimusc in shock absorbing doses.

After a good ten minutes passed, the rashes started to go away. I could hear people sigh around me in relief. Ruslan arrived but could not say a thing. He just stood there shocked by what he saw.

Nail's face, lips, ears, and limbs were still swollen, so the doctors prescribed further treatments. Then one by one, they left us. Nail conquered death for the second time within one hour. During the afternoon, the swelling went away slowly, and after ten to twelve hours, Nail turned back into a boy with an angel's face. I was filled with exhaustion and sadness. It took a real effort to even speak. When he finally went to sleep, I could at last cry for a bit, which eased my pains somewhat.

In the evening, I phoned home, and Ruslan told me that his mother's blood pressure was still above 200 so she couldn't come in, and that after today he wouldn't take my place during the nights because he was afraid. I understood both of them.

During the evening visitation, the doctor was relieved to see that Nail was sleeping peacefully. They left our room, and I got up to shut the door behind them. I heard the nurse's question involuntarily: "But why didn't you move him up to the ICU?"

"Because we couldn't have made it in time. Every syndrome was showing save for the laryngeal edema. The child would have suffocated within two minutes."

Well, I wouldn't wish that night on anyone.

In the morning, I woke sleepy, dizzy and in a bad mood. I couldn't decide what to do with the erring nurse. On the one hand, I knew that she had a family, small children and she only did what she did out of negligence. On the other hand, she almost killed a child accidentally. My child.

I imagined multiple times what I would say to her if she entered the room to apologize. The first variants were quite savage, but with every re-imagination of the situation, my anger grew smaller. In the end, I was content with telling her never to be so irresponsible and clumsy in the future. For me what was most important was that Nail was alive, and the triumph I felt from that could suppress any other pain.

The almost fatal accident, of course, became a popular conversation topic in the department as many people unwillingly witnessed what had happened. As a result, many parents got spooked and went into a mild panic, which I thought was completely understandable. I told anybody who asked me about what had happened adhering to the facts without any over dramatization. In fact none of the doctors, only some parents and nurses, were curious about the details.

I was still under the effect of the previous day when in the morning, the guilty nurse stormed into our room. She completely disarmed me with this unexpected move. Before I could speak, she started shouting at me – not caring that I had Nail in my arms – calling me all kinds of names. She was spitting hate at me, and her head became a red flaming fireball. I never expected such strong emotions from her. She just kept shouting that I was spreading rumors and getting her in trouble when she was only trying to save my son's life. That she instantly fetched the emergency tray to administer the lifesaving drugs if the doctors didn't make it in time. Allegedly, she had already prepared a syringe.

"What, you thought I would have let him die?" she snarled. "Injecting DIFA is not rocket science, and in these situations, a nurse can do it too."

"Is that so? And you had the audacity to run off before waiting to see whether he would survive?"

"I already saw that he was getting better."

"That's interesting. You could have told that to the other doctors and the adjunct because they remained for at least another fifteen minutes to make sure the child didn't suffocate. Then they could have left. But, of course, you had to hurry to catch your bus."

"I did my work without error, and I won't stand and be accused and insulted by you."

"You only forgot to ask for a doctor's assistance in a critical situation."

"I was preparing the emergency tray. What part of that don't you understand?"

"If your colleague didn't come in at that moment and ask for help, Nail wouldn't be among us today. Maybe you wouldn't be either… What you did disgusts me, and I feel a deep pity toward you. You tried to save your own skin when a child's life was hanging in the balance, and you don't even feel ashamed. I ask you never to set foot in this room again, and keep your filthy black nails from my child's infusion set."

"I'll tell the professor and the head nurse right now about the filth you keep spreading about me. You'll regret this!" Then she ran off crying.

I was shaking from anger, and it took a great deal of restraint not to go after her and beat her. But Nail held me back because I didn't dare to leave him alone even for a moment.

After this particular incident, I felt that I had divided the opinions of both the parents and the nurses. There were some who believed me and some who believed her. I didn't want to waste my energy on persuading people to support my opinion, but she tried to besmirch me on every possible forum. Even the cleaning lady – with whom we always had a good relationship – noted that I was not my old self anymore and that my "eyes have opened." Like those and those – she nodded toward the two neighboring rooms – and I knew what she meant. Anybody who dared to say anything had always been instantly hated on the department. Some of the parents had been living in this madness, in the shadow of death for several years. At first I did not agree with their methods. I thought what they did went a step too far, but time has proven they were right. From this moment on, I respected and admired their courage.

I could dedicate more to the stories of the other patients. Their stories could fill an entire book themselves. Because everybody who went through this – no matter how fate ends their tale – is a hero. And not only here but anywhere, in every other city, country or continent.

The ones I knew personally were all great kids, wonderful children with superhuman wills to live. Some of them are still fighting. Some have won or at least they have for now. Others were defeated by this terrible disease.

Many times, I see their smart looks. I hear their childish chatting. I see the tears and the wrinkles of agonies on their faces.

I hear them crying out in revolution, the ringing of the chains that constrict their weak bodies more and more. Then I see them dissolved into atoms when their soul gives itself up to the end, and the body is left alone in a futile fight. Their looks become empty, the sounds are not heard, and nothing and no one matters anymore. It's getting dark. There's only a glimmer of light left, a torch far away; everything else has faded into the dark. A sweet melody beckons from closer and closer, fills their souls with a heavenly breath and the desire to fall asleep.

I can't think of anything sadder than a child's death. It's one of my most painful life experiences – after the loss of my own child – hearing the silent screams of other parents and grandparents wailing beside their children.

I miss them.

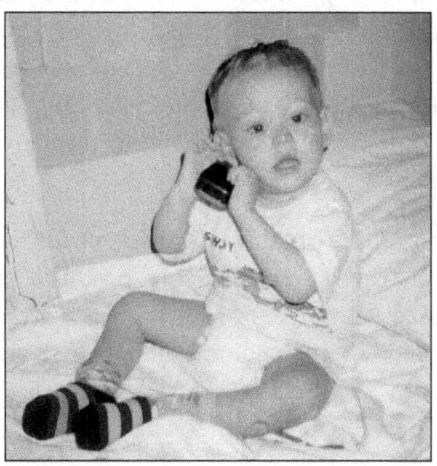

Nail with a mobile phone chained to the hospital bed

The nurse kept her promise. They told the treating doctors who visited us together after visitation. They did not reproach me; they only smiled. They didn't ask what had happened. They only told me to believe that the nurse was innocent. According to them, Nail simply went into anaphylactic shock, which was not entirely unexpected. I watched them leave and became confused – I didn't understand anything.

Why did they judge the situation without asking my opinion? Why were they not interested in what I'd heard and seen? What I saw, I saw with my own eyes. Am I not the mother of the child? Of the child who had almost died in that simple little shock?

This was the moment when I understood that in the thick of battle, we could only rely on ourselves. Because for everybody else, Nail was just a clinical case, a piece of statistics, a medical history without a name, face, or personality. For us he was the light of our eyes. There is a big difference between the two.

Nail was unbelievably pale. By evening, he had a fever again. His throat and gum hurt, and his swollen eyes could still be seen after twenty-four hours. They started him on a more effective combined antibiotics and antifungal treatment.[16] The following day, he received blood twice. The fever that started a day after his shock only went down after a week. By that time, we jointly managed to get a handle on his penis situation. The mucus in his mouth was treated by pioctanin and lapis while I applied various oils.

I talked to Laci and Gyöngyi multiple times on the phone. I tried to look back calmly on the past days. According to Laci, death had shown me his face on that day. Gyöngyi thought that the heavens were protecting us, warning us beforehand that they were looking out for us. I thought that Nail had become immortal – if he lived through this, he could live through anything.

The next afternoon, while Ruslan was watching over Nailka's dreams, I ran out into the city to acquire new medicinal products as well as to restock the ones we had used up. While the food such as bio-bread, cereals, salads, juices and teas could be obtained and prepared by my aunt and Ruslan, I could not delegate these to them. I had a long list and read through everything before deciding on whether a particular product could make it into our repertoire.

After the practical applications of a vegetarian diet, juice treatment, reflexology and aromatherapy, I turned my attention toward more irrational branches.

I went into the bookshop selling esoteric literature, one of my favorite places. Here I always found delicacies that suited me. I knew Ibolya, the saleswoman, well by sight. She always encouraged me not to give up the search because help would come eventually. My eyes settled on a book that was about colors, more specifically the application of colors in therapy. "Aura soma" is a color combination made from dyed lotus oil dreamed up by an Irish woman who later went blind. For each duet of colors, there is a different spiritual explanation. Usually people choose one instinctively, which is to say the bottle finds its owner. But I wanted one for Nail, so I remained undecided. By Ibolya's recommendation, I chose the nr.20 "child-saver" bottle.

I immediately gave Nail the pink-colorless (crystal color) composite. He really enjoyed it. He kept shaking them together, but the colors arranged

---

16. Vancomícin (aka Vancomycin), Tienam (aka Primaxin), Amphotericin

themselves back so one was always above the other. They always found balance. According to the method, it has to be within view of the patient so it can attract attention. I put it on the TV opposite the bed. Nail adored it and frequently asked for it. Sometimes he dropped it on the stone floor, but the glass proved to be shock resistant. I didn't want to take it away, because then what was the point of buying it? I let Nail and the bottle sync up, and sometimes I rubbed it against his temple. At these times, I kept playing with it with my hands and got the impression that I was holding a rosary.

Then another day, Nail asked for the bottle again. He played with it and then stood up on his bed; with an intentional motion, he threw it on the ground. But the vial didn't directly hit the floor. It smashed against the metal railing of his bed and broke in two. Again, it lasted only a few seconds. Like a dagger through my heart, a sudden fear enveloped me, and in an instant, a thought formed in my mind: "Nail rejects the child-saver bottle. He doesn't need it." But as soon as the thought surfaced, I was already trying to wipe it from my memory like cleaning a blackboard with a wet sponge. But I couldn't wipe away the fear. I picked up the remains and put them in the table. Then I took Nail in my arms and started consoling him that everything would be fine. And he was completely calm.

I immersed myself more and more in the world of healing colors and sounds.

I read about the healing properties of gold and peach colors and wanted to make some pillowcases for Nail, but sitting there in the hospital, I had no way to obtain or sew them. I talked to my Italian friend, Lella, and she mobilized her family in Bormio. Within two days, three pillowcases were completed and posted: one peach, one gold, and one old gold-colored. Nail chose the peach one. He often held the cool, silk-like material close to him in the summer heat.

We bought a cassette player and a large quantity of beautiful soul calming music tapes. Ones titled the "Forest Song", the "Song of the Sea", "Dance of Dolphins and Whales", "Crystal Silence", "Songs of White Mountains", etc. The music didn't just affect us. The little girl Lilla in the next room also came to love the sounds of dolphins.

When we were alone with Nail during evenings, we turned on the relaxing music and tried to forget the day's strife.

On the 21st of June, we could go home again. As they found that his potassium levels were too low, the doctors gave us some[17] to have at home and asked us to feed him bananas. That salty concoction was not easy for him to swallow, so we had to employ a few tricks.

In retrospect, these two weeks were the happiest times of our treatment. We could spend five days at home away from the smell of disinfectants and medicine, hospital schedules, infusions and needle pokes.

We only had to go back for two days when they continued their treatment according to the protocol.

The home that offered a return to our previous life filled us all up with energy. In an instant, I became very active and tireless. I collected more and more information on the most well-known alternative cancer treatment: the Gerson-therapy. I wanted to identify the transitions and overlaps between macrobiotics and the Gerson-method. My position was that in themselves none of them would be enough for Nail; because of his young age, we could create deficiency diseases and weaken his immune system. I wanted to learn the principles of the diet and understand the main prohibitions. To tailor it to Nail and, if needed, expand them.

Macrobiotics originated in Japan and is renowned in curing cancer. Their believers say that eating a bowl of brown rice a day won't cure anybody. Much more is needed. Any factors that could disturb the still weak, healing body had to be cut, including holidays, travel, overexertion and exhaustion. The basis of the diet is cereals, vegetables, and oily seeds.

In contrast, the Gerson-diet is based on the method of a former German-Jewish doctor, Dr. Max Gerson. The essence of the method is that by actively detoxifying the body, we make it more resistant. If it is successful, then the cancerous process stops, and the tumor gets absorbed or encapsulated, so it's becomes safe to remove.

The diet lasts years and is a very hard trial. Only the most determined patients can stand the Spartan conditions. This determination can mostly be found in cancer patients, so the main successes come from this area, many times even on patients in the withering period. Probably it would have even more success with patients not so far gone.

---

17. (2,0), KCL injection

During the first semester, the patient can only eat vegetarian food. They have to give up milk and egg products too. Every day, every hour, they have to drink a glass (so twelve to thirteen in total) of raw vegetable or fruit juice (carrot, salad, paprika, red cabbage, parsley, cress, watercress, apple).

A cancer patient can never be hungry. Aside from the juices, they have to eat three times a day and drink great amounts of mint tea. For breakfast, they usually get porridge, boiled dried fruits (both boiled in water), orange juice and bananas. For lunch and dinner, it's a raw salad and a vegetable soup that Hippocrates himself prescribed for his patients ("Let your food be your medicine and your medicine be your food."), fried potatoes with steamed vegetables and fresh fruit. A teaspoon of flax oil, lemon water, and garlic paste can be used as spices daily.

The basic rule of the Gerson-diet is: 0% salt, 0% chemicals, and 0% fat (except for the flax oil). The diet is very rich in potassium but low in sodium, protein, and fat.

Another part of detoxification is the enema that's to be applied five to six times a day prepared from a 1-4 ratio mixture of coffee solution made from chemical free coffee-beans. It has to be done lying on the right side to facilitate the detoxification effects of the liver. Supposedly, it's also a very good pain reliever.

In the beginning, Dr. Gerson lost many of his patients to hepatic coma. Back then he didn't know how important it was to remove toxins from the body regularly by enemas and juices. Both of them can be dangerous if done separately.

For the cleansing of the bowels, they prescribe purgation every two days by using castor oil.

The appearance of healing reactions is a good thing and part of the treatment. Such as fever, which shows that the immune system is not completely damaged, but vomiting, headaches, loss of appetite, swelling can also occur. These symptoms usually disappear within three days.

Its medicines usually contain natural ingredients such as thyroid and pancreas extracts, potassium, hydrochloric acid, pepsin, B1 and B6 vitamins, Lugol solution, Coenzyme Q-10, niacin, royal jelly, flax oil, castor oil and unique veal-liver capsules and injections.

The therapy is usually applied for at least one and a half years.

Both macrobiotics and the Gerson-diet have holistic views. Holistics is not the same as the alternative treatment, and the two should not be confused. The main principle of holistics is that the whole is greater than the sum of its parts. Starting from this, it tries to know and treat the patient's body, soul, emotions and intellect.

I only shared the essence of the Gerson-method with you because it took me so much time and energy to learn it.

The Gerson-method – according to my convictions – is very effective. Nail was reborn by it, and we only did it for two months.

If you are interested or have nothing to lose, don't give up. Find a reliable doctor who's cooperative and obtain all information. If you can't find bio-products, peel the fruits and vegetables well, and if you can't buy a press for hundreds of dollars, get a fruit-centrifuge, but try it… You can find all the ingredients to prepare an enema: Q10 capsule, flax oil, vitamins, garlic, mint, castor oil, potassium, royal jelly and bio-bread can all be bought in Hungary and various countries around the world.

You can find the latest information on the Internet, or you can phone them or send mail to the following address (you need the final report in English):

The Gerson Institute
P.O. Box #161358
San Diego, CA 92176
http://gerson.org/gerpress/

Be persistent. Based on the first final report, the staff of the Gerson Institute (not the clinic; that's in Mexico) get back to you and tell you about the chance they think the patient has for recovery. If despite this, someone insists on admittance, they won't send them away.

In Hungary, Beata Bishop made this method known. Her book describing her experiences can be bought through the Egészségforrás Foundation.

I started giving Nail enemas regularly, but I decided to do one or two per day. I bought bio-coffee, but I diluted it in 1/20 ratio instead of ¼ to protect his heart. With any method I judged dangerous, I applied the principles of homeopathy: very, very big-ratio dilution. Many times, I administered the enema with chamomile tea instead of coffee. These enemas shocked me more than once. But in the end, they proved to be not as bad as I had expected. My mother-in-law brought a bulb, a "pear" from Moscow that I used to give Nail enemas. His little legs had to be held out, and he needed to be talked to. It became sort of a family activity where Ruslan and Csingiz alternatingly entertained him. I oiled the bulb well and squirted many small amounts of liquid into his colon. What was shocking was many times what came out was the remains of meals several weeks or months before. Then, I always wondered how all this became lodged in the colon for weeks at a time when Nail had been on detoxifying diets for a long time.

I only stopped the enemas once when his thrombocytes measured really low because I was afraid that a possible burst capillary could cause problems with his coagulation.

I always had a mad enthusiasm for my children. I fear for Csingiz on account of his recklessness, but it's also the main reason I adore him. By the way, it can't be easy to live with such a name – the Russian equivalent of Genghis Khan. He's proved this many times since his birth. Nail was the polar opposite. There wasn't a fierce warrior inside him but rather a peacemaker. There was something astonishingly wonderful in this. Despite his age of only one and a half years, I sometimes had the definite impression that Nail was several thousand years old. I felt the wisdom in his eyes, his skin. And I'm not talking about some learned superhuman intelligence or talent. I can't even use words to describe what I mean by this. He simply emanated this wisdom – for lack of a better word – without ever speaking a word. What's more, most of the time I felt this when he was asleep.

When we shared a moment together, I told him how wise he was.

"Please," I begged him. "Stay with me. This is why you have to stay… I need your wisdom. I'm lost without you. You need to stay here and teach us everything. Once I've learned everything, I want you to be proud of me. Get well, my darling. I love you, son. I love you…"

I know… It was a feeble attempt. I fooled myself and tried to fool him as well just to make him stay for a while, although I knew that I didn't have the right to force him to stay. This is not how it works, but I wanted to believe. And I loved him more than anybody else in this whole world.

Before Csingiz was born, I wanted a son, and I wanted my son to resemble his father. God listened to my prayers. With Nail, it was completely different.

I was dreaming of a beautiful, charming little girl with huge blue eyes and curly fair hair. Just like a little angel. Ruslan was not sure about whether he wanted a second child after Csingiz was born. He said we should wait.

But I wanted this child so much. I prayed to God all night for a daughter. And finally, my prayers were answered.

Csingiz and I were coming home for Easter from Moscow. Ruslan had to stay in Russia for his training. When I was sure about becoming a mom again, I called Ruslan. First, he was not amused.

Later on, he became enthusiastic. Everyone predicted that I was pregnant with a girl. I even bought a few pink dresses and used to call my baby to be "Dzsami." (We picked the name Dzsmila Csenge for her.)

I was thirty weeks pregnant when we had to come home with Csingiz again. By this time, I'd decided to give birth to my child in Hungary. The next ultrasound scan clearly determined the gender of my child. I was having a boy.

My husband and my mother-in-law were happy to hear my great news when I called them. Our next task was to pick a name for our son. Ruslan suggested the name "Rinát." This had been my favorite until he recommended another one: Nail.

Csingiz fell in love with this name. He didn't even want to consider anything else but insisted on this one. And we respected his wish.

The birth was scheduled on 10th, 24th and finally, the 31st of December. His head looked huge on the ultrasound scan. I got scared a bit. Nothing happened. I didn't even have any labor pain, and the scan calculated the baby's weight to be around 5 kg (11.02 lbs.).

Finally, it turned out to be quite accurate. Nail was born on 3rd January with a natural, unmedicated vaginal birth, with 5280 grams (11.6 lbs.).

Nail grew rapidly. He weighed 11.5 kg (25.35 lbs.) when he was just seven months old. He was a strong, big baby with little teeth coming early and hadn't been sick.

The only worrisome sign was that he was late to start walking. His was not the best in balancing himself while walking, but with a little assistance, he cruised along furniture. In March, he got the flu. At the end of the month, he was sick again. His temperature was high, and his cough was not improving. Besides these symptoms, he was a happy and energetic child.

In June, we started to write a diary about Nail. It was a wonderful way to record the life and memories. It also helped to record Nail's growth and progress. It was useful to identify challenges with our child's behavior and our parenting skills and write about how we are handling them. This parenting journal helped me express the emotions I felt as a parent and provide a healthy outlet for me to deal with those emotions. Later, it took a long time for me to open this diary… On the first page of "Nail's Diary," there was a quote.

In June, we had to leave our room in the hospital and move to the adjoining room. We shared the place with Gergő, an almost four-year-old boy. He had been sick for two years. He had chemotherapy and a bone marrow transplant, but a few months later, his neuroblastoma returned. They have been living in this room for quite a long time, and they lived far away from the cancer center, in another county.

Gergő was a smart boy. He knew a lot of poems and rhymes. All he wanted was to go to kindergarten and play with the other kids. But there was little chance for him to realize this dream.

We needed to compromise a lot because we were not alone. We had to share the room, we had to share the pain, and we had to share the sorrow. Sometimes I feel sorry that I haven't realized that Gergő's condition was gradually deteriorating. Until the last moment, I've been waiting for someone to come and save him. I've been waiting for a miracle…

I didn't want to become aware of the fact that I could lose my son. I overrated every positive sign and tried to ignore the negative ones. I was extremely afraid of facing my own fears.

Then one day, I stopped by an antique book shop where I found a poetry book about fairies. I thought Gergő would love that book since he was always talking about spring fairy and summer fairy.

Before I gave it to him, I copied a poem on the first page of Nail's Diary.

> "WINDFLOWER
> *Even if the weather is harsh outside*
> *And it may be hard to believe*
> *That spring will arrive*
> *Chasing winter away*
> *Windflower believes in the light*
> *And the spring to come*
> *And make the cold winter belate*
> *Bringing vernal blossoms*
> *For those who have faith."*

Isn't it beautiful?

On 30th June, I wrote the following in the diary:

"Nailka is fine. Thank God.

He is walking rather quickly while holding onto furniture. He is taking his first steps without help. His appetite is good. He is trying to repeat our words. We've been here at home for three days now. I have a lot of things to do. It's 1 a.m. Dad was here today and assembled the shelves. Everything falls into place. Csingiz loves riding his bike. I'm afraid he'll fall. Nail plays with Lego pieces and his stuffed animals. Sometimes he's having minor pain.

In the morning I gave him some fruit on an empty stomach. For dinner, he ate a little more fruit and bio bean soup with whole meal pasta. I put some ground cumin (remedy for bloating) and sour cabbage juice (remedy for lactic acid) in it. And a few drops just like in the morning.

In the afternoon, I gave him yogurt with egg yolk and a teaspoon of olive oil.

In the evening, he wanted some cherries, a little soup, and yogurt. Drops, as usual.

Late at night, I performed an enema on him with coffee solution. A lot of fecal matter exited."

At 1 a.m., my day wasn't over. I took a book from the shelf and began to read about the life of healer Edgar Cayce. According to him, healing can only occur if we connect our mind and body, if we are able to encourage the healing process. Every little cell of our body is the universe. There is no death. All of our lives are learning and gaining experience.

Edgar Cayce was a simple man. He didn't even use or understand medical terminology. He always used plain language when addressing his readers. He believed that tumors are caused by the accumulation of waste products in our body. He suggested different types of diets for those with sarcoma or melanoma, containing a lot of vegetables like carrots, beetroot, watermelon or plantain tea. He diagnosed each and every patient individually. Depending on the type of the tumor, he recommended certain diets to strengthen the lymphatic or the digestive system. As for prevention, he advised to eat a piece of raw almond a day.

On 3rd July, Nail had another forty-eight hour long treatment.[18] Almost everything went as planned. We could forget about L-asparaginase due to the serious allergic reaction it caused last time.

By the second day of the treatment, Nailka's temperature has risen, and I tried to cool his little body gradually. I didn't want the doctors to give him Algopyrin – I wanted Nailka to fight. I believe that fever is a natural response by the body and is part of the healing process. Nail proved to be a great partner in letting me raise his temperature and then gradually reduce it. I think we managed to kill a lot of cancer cells with this method.

On 6th July, we were allowed to go home. We were so happy to hear that we were supposed to take Nail to hospital only for the treatments and then spend the afternoons and nights at home.

I felt we lived just like a normal family again, at least for these few weeks. I was given an illusion of a future that never happened. I was happy. We were happy. Together. Time seemed to slow down for us. There was a strange glow in Nailka's eyes. I didn't realize what it was, but he smiled at us a million times during these weeks. I believed that the glow, the smiles, the hugs, the cheerful afternoons were signs of further steps in his recovery.

He was fascinated by vehicles. Ruslan spent hours with him walking on the street and naming every type of cars that drove by. I think he was ready to leave but hadn't decided which way to go.

---

[18]. High dose ARA-C treatment. Eye pain, tearing, sensitivity to light and blurred vision may occur with high-dose therapy. Often steroid drops or ointment (Nailka was given Ultracortenol) to the eyes are used to prevent or relieve this condition. He was also given Zofran.

At the end of the street, there was an old, rusty jeep called JUMBO parked in the garden under the shades of trees. This old yellow car mesmerized Nailka every time we passed by the fence.

He also loved planes and ships – just like his brother, Csingiz. They used to immerse themselves in a picture book about the Titanic and build never-ending railroads on the carpet of their room.

Nailka loved puttering around in the garden, picking cherry tomatoes, apricots and grapes. He was running around all the time, wanted to see and smell and experience the whole world. Like he had known that there was not much time left to enjoy life.

During the breaks between the chemotherapies, we visited the hospital for short antibiotic treatments. I tried to spend as little time as possible among the thrilling walls.

We were living in two different worlds – at home and in the clinic. They were completely different. I always felt insecure, tired, and worried when we had to enter the door of the hospital. At home, I was happy, cheerful, and full of hope. I wanted to distance myself from the cruelties of the institute and never thought about these sick little children passing away. I forced myself into an illusion.

Closing my eyes makes me invisible.

That's what children do.

Nailka's daily treatments were not that short, by the way. They should've taken not more than thirty minutes, but we always had to wait for a doctor to start the treatment, then for another one to close the cannula, and we were just waiting for long, long hours…

One day I was sitting in the waiting room with Nail in my hands. It was already 2: 30 p.m. I felt anger, and I couldn't bear to stay for any long in this place. I burst into tears. We've been punished for my outburst: Nail was the last to be treated that day.

Healthcare workers didn't always realize that sometimes we need just a little smile, a touch on the shoulder, or a few encouraging words.

Based on the literature, I decided to skip soy and fried meals from Nail's diet. I knew that this mono-diet would be challenging, but we needed to take this step to reach the remission phase.

I bought milk thistle seed. It has positive effects on the liver. Its antioxidant compound reduces free radical production and oxidative damage. It may also inhibit the binding of toxins to the liver. It has been shown to have positive effects on alcoholic liver disease, hepatitis, and toxin-induced liver problems as well. In order to make it easier for Nail to swallow, I ground the seeds and mixed them with his yogurt.

Cayce recommended peanut oil massage for the head in the mornings. He described this ingredient as a food for the nerves and muscular forces. I rubbed a small portion of oil into Nailka's scalp each morning. It had at least one beneficial effect: Nailka didn't lose his hair.

One morning, Nail was very pale, and I discovered blood spots all over his body. They must have been so-called "platelet spots." I had heard about this symptom a lot. It was due to a low platelet count. He was not bothered by the spots at all. He was playful during the day and ate a lot of spinach, corn on the cob, and pasta with garlic and broccoli.

The day of July 9th – another milestone in our story that almost caused me a heart attack.

We went to hospital for the antibiotic treatment as usual. I reported the "platelet spots" to the doctor on duty. She drew blood from Nail and sent it to the lab for testing. After the treatment,[19] Nail was eating his dinner of parsley potatoes cheerfully when the doctor entered the room.

"We're having a little problem," she said, pointing her finger at the lab tests results she was holding. "I'm afraid we need to send Nail up to the ICU."

"What? Why? What happened?"

"The results show that he has a very high concentration of potassium in his blood. It's 7.5. We need to act fast. This high level can cause his heart to stop."

I looked at my son, who was eating his meal, and I couldn't spot any dangerous signs. I was surprised, and I didn't understand what was happening.

"This is weird," I said, still looking surprised. "A few weeks ago, his potassium level was very low. We were even prescribed frequent oral doses to achieve higher concentration."

---

19. It was a five-day long Rocephin treatment.

"Okay, I understand. But now, please go to the ICU," she insisted. "In the meantime, I will talk to one of my colleagues since Nail's blood test results are quite disturbing. I'm ordering the platelet products."[20]

I followed the doctor's orders without further hesitation, but I could feel my heart beat in my throat. I was really scared.

I've never been to the ICU before. As I entered the door with my son still chewing on the last bites of his dinner, I was surprised to see the cleanliness and order up here. The tiles were shining. The whole corridor was quiet. I was moving slowly with my son in one hand and the infusion bottle in the other. I was afraid that his heart would stop at any minute. I wanted to cry. I wanted to scream and shout, but it wasn't the right place or time.

I heard a lot about the ICU from the other parents. They said that they had a wonderful and professional team.

One of our acquaintances from here in the hospital, Viki, has been hospitalized with meningitis and has been treated at the ICU. She was a cancer patient. The little girl had severe pain; therefore, the doctors decided to put her into a medically induced coma. It was heartbreaking to hear her parents taking turns at the side of her bed.

We didn't know whether Viki would ever wake up from the coma. I still remember the paralyzing feeling. Everyone in the oncology rooted for this family.

I will never forget the day when her mother, Hajni, roamed into the oncology and shouted in tears: "She is awake. My daughter came out of the coma, and she is fine! Oh, my God!"

It happened two years ago, but it is still a disturbingly touching memory. We cried together with Hajni and celebrated the success story of the ICU.

I needed to put Nail into his bed. He began to cry. The doctor injected a diuretic drug[21] into his infusion set and drew additional blood samples from his vein.

I was scared. Meanwhile, Csingiz and Ruslan went to the bath of the city to cool themselves by swimming on this hot summer day. They suspected nothing about what was happening with Nail.

---

20. I checked the lab test, and it showed critical results: white blood cells 600, hemoglobin 68 g/L, hematocrit 18, platelet 10,000 /μl.
21. Furon

Sanyi came over from the adjacent room where his son, Gergő, was lying.

"What happened?" he asked.

"I don't know exactly." My voice trembled. "They said that his potassium level is too high, and his heart could stop at any minute. But look at him. I can't believe this."

"Ah. Nothing serious," Sanyi said waving his hand. "He's going to fine, believe me."

I was thankful for his understanding and nice words. Honestly, I learned a lot from Sanyi and his wife. They never let their child alone. One of them was always watching Gergő. Nights and days merged into one continuous grayness. They were sitting on the side of Gergő's deathbed and guarded him until the end.

One of the most moving experiences of my life was to watch these two parents lose their son without being able to help him.

I'm not going to talk about this family or any other family in detail due to privacy. But I felt I had to incorporate their story into Nailka's because we were so close.

Thirty minutes later, the doctor came back for more blood. Soon we got a call from the lab that, according to the blood tests, Nail's potassium level was 3.61, which is completely normal, and the former faulty test reports must have been a mistake.

It was such a relief to hear that, but at the same time, I was disappointed to realize that such mistakes can happen.

The three units of platelets arrived. I was surprised to see that it was an RH negative blood, but Nail had RH positive. The doctor said they ran out of the latter. I was scared that the different type of blood might cause harm to my son, but the doctor ensured me that everything would be all right. We didn't have time to wait for additional blood units because Nail's platelet number dropped under 10,000.

After the procedure, we went back to our room at the oncology. Since the diuretic substance tends to increase the flow of urine, the doctor instructed me to give Nail drinks regularly, and she also decided to speed up the infusion. She was very helpful and understanding when I insisted that Nail needed to get his red blood cell product during the night. She gave permission for the treatment, and I was sitting next to my son's bed all night long watching the RBC product slowly dripping into his body.

The next morning, no one mentioned our visit at the ICE by mistake although I'm sure everyone knew it. Probably they thought it was just another lecture for the parents; they were certainly having those kinds of experiences on a daily basis – not a big deal. But they were wrong. It wasn't natural at all, and it made me very scared.

Nail's blood test results showed only a little improvement.[22]

I put him into his bed and rushed out to the toilet. He started playing with his puzzle. A few minutes later when I returned, I saw a horrific sight. Nail was kneeling on the side of his bed in the middle of a pool of blood. His central venous cannula broke, and his blood was dripping down on the bed. The infusion set was hanging next to him disconnected.

A nurse heard my shouting and came into our room.

Fortunately, the situation was not as horrific as it seemed. The nurse investigated the cannula and said that it could be replaced easily without an operation. She cleaned the bed and tried to calm me.

I was sitting on the side of the bed watching my son sleeping quietly. I was sad and scared at the same time and began to cry.

"WHY?" I whispered, wiping off my tears.

We were allowed to go home in the afternoon. I fell into my bed exhausted and slept like a stone until late next morning. I woke up feeling weary and grouchy. I quarreled with my husband over something irrelevant. We were both stressed out.

By Friday, Nail's whole body has been full of blood spots again. I applied poultices to the bigger lesions on his leg, but I knew that it wouldn't be enough to fight back against the side effects of chemotherapy.

A few days earlier, I read about the benefits of alfalfa. Thanks to its high level of vitamin K, alfalfa sprouts can help symptoms related to chemotherapy and can be used as a nutritional supplement. I prepared a

---

22. His platelet number was still very low (18,000); therefore, the doctors ordered four more units of platelets. Again, just HR products arrived. I wasn't happy about it, but I had to accept the situation.

fresh salad from bio alfalfa and also an herbal tincture using high-proof alcohol just to make sure that I'd have additional reserve for the winter.

I was worried about the long dark months of winter. Organic fruits and vegetables can be much more expensive during the winter and, perhaps, harder to find. But now we still had everything: green beans, potato, zucchini, spinach, parsley. I used all of these for Nailka's daily Hippocrates soup. I knew that I had to think forward to the winter months when there wouldn't be enough fresh ingredients for his diet. We could have used a freezer, but we'd been up to our ears in debt and couldn't afford it. Our company was left without control, and we'd been taking out a lot of money for Nail's treatment. Finally, we'd lost our suppliers due to our delayed payments. We were just one step away from total bankruptcy. We couldn't pay our taxes and monthly installments.

After long quarrels and apologies, my parents' house was put up for mortgage as a final solution. We used the loan to pay off another. I didn't care because Nail meant more than anything to me. I knew that we'd have our difficulties straightened out once Nailka got better.

On Sunday evening, I noticed a bleeding hematoma inside Nail's mouth. I got scared, and I had to decide whether we should wait until the morning or go to hospital immediately. I chose to stay home and pay attention to every little sign. Probably, the doctor on duty wouldn't have ordered platelets for Nail during the night.

The main reason behind my choice was that Nailka looked fine. I thought that it would be wiser not to expose my child to negative stress unnecessarily – just like in the ominous case late time at the ICU.

For the first time ever, I believed in myself and in my decision.

I took responsibility for that night.

I went out to the kitchen to make an herb-infused balm. I used honey, purple coneflower, Calcimusc, vitamin C and a pinch of baking soda. I applied this balm on his mouth every hour. I fell asleep next to my son around 3 a.m.

In the morning, we rushed into hospital for control. Nail's blood test was horrible,[23] and he had a high fever again. The doctors ordered four units

---

23. The number of platelets decreased to 13,000. The extremely low number of white blood cells suggested that he became more susceptible to infections.

of platelets – from his blood type this time. The number of platelets had tripled by next morning.

I walked a little in the garden. I watched the full moon and tried to interpret its thousand years' old secrets. I found myself praying to the Virgin Mary. I begged her to save Balázs and Gergő.

On July 20th, there was no fever, but Nail's appetite hasn't returned yet. In the afternoon, the results of the blood tests of July 5th arrived. All negative.

During the daily visits, I asked the doctors to stop one of Nailka's medicines, the Amikin for infections. They agreed. I didn't want to needlessly poison my son. His body had to concentrate on recovery. A bit later, a nurse came in holding an Amikin injection in her hand. She was grumpy and rude.

I didn't like her because the other day, she had roamed into the department laughing and waking up the children. She wasn't on duty that night and probably was heading to a party judging by her miniskirt and heavy makeup. Her colleagues tried to calm her down. Let me put it this way: she was not the best nurse. But I don't want to generalize.

Most of the nurses at the oncology understood us patients and parents. They had myriad of responsibilities, and their job could be very difficult sometimes. We all knew it. As a mother of a sick child, all I needed was respect and good-heartedness.

But this grumpy lady was not that type. She injected the drug into my son's bottle and left the room in a hurry. *I will not leave it at that*, I thought. So I went to find the doctor on duty and tell him what happened. He had given me the truth and ordered the nurse to change the infusion set.

I couldn't wait to get home.

Nailka had shown fantastic improvements. He learned to walk around the house on his own. That was incredible. He took three or four steps at once and also learned balancing. I was full of joy. We all understood the importance of this improvement, which we interpreted as a step in his recovery.

On the morning of July 24th, I saw a crowd standing in front of the building of the oncology. I saw sad eyes on bitter faces. I realized that a terrible thing must have happened.

Balázska passed away around 6:45 in the morning.

Even though I saw him at the ICU, lying helplessly…

Even though I heard him shouting for weeks…

Even though we knew that this would happen but still…

I didn't understand the reason. The reason behind his death. The reason behind his illness.

Why? Why? Why?

Why him? And why Gergő and Lilla? Why Nail and all the others?

What was his sin? And what was our sin?

On what basis is it decided whether they stay or leave?

Who knows the answer? The *real* answer.

The answer to the question why and how.

This is the most unfair thing about life.

Since April, this was the first death here at the oncology. Two boys had passed away at home, but none of our little patients died here in the hospital. I knew little about Gergő. He had been transported to another facility for bone marrow transplantation by the time we arrived and started Nail's therapy. I didn't know him but heard a lot about him and his parents. I know their painful journey to the valley of death. I respect them for their strength and toughness. I realized that I can't close my eyes anymore.

Ruslan was devastated to hear the bad news. In the following days, we tried to concentrate on Nail's condition and recovery, but we felt distracted and confused. We acknowledged the nearness of death, and we were scared about losing the most precious thing in this world, our son.

Nail's treatment[24] continued on Tuesday. They performed bone marrow biopsy and lumbar puncture on him.

After the long day, I tried to calm my son down with a lavender foot bath and a massage.

---

24. Our treatment followed the protocol of block "OCTADD" of Interfant-98. He also got steroids and cytostatics, VCR, DRB, ARA-C and MTX.

July 26th is a legendary day in our diary. I'll never forget those moments. During the afternoon visit, the professor's phone rang, and he went out to the corridor. His voice echoed in the silent corridor. I could hear that they were talking about Nail's test results. I heard joy in his voice. I began to cry.

He hung up the phone and came back to the room. He touched my shoulder and said: "I just got a call from the pathology. I have amazing news. Nail's bone marrow is clear. That's remission. He's on the right path now…"

I saw the smile on his face. He took a pen out of his pocket, went to the end of the bed and wrote something on Nail's temperature chart. I checked the note after he had left. It was one word: *remissio*. It meant everything to us.

I was still crying when Ruslan arrived. First, he thought that something bad happened. When I told him the big news, I saw the happy tears in his eyes. Even the nurse on duty was moved by the fantastic change in Nailka's condition.

I had to run out to the city to tell everyone about the miracle. While I was running to my mother's, I made the streets wet with my tears of joy. My mother cried with me.

That night I wrote the following words in my diary, with all capital letters: "He's in excellent condition, although eats less because of the heat.

TODAY our marrow tests came back negative.

He has less than 5% cancerous cells.

This is one of the happiest days of my life.

We have to believe, he's already on the path of healing.

They closed up Nail at noon, and he's been walking around freely all afternoon.

He slept 3.5 hours during the day."

We were in the middle of a four-day ARA-C treatment. As usual, his temperature started to rise. It was already around 102°F, but I didn't mind. I didn't give him any antipyretics. I rather chose cold packs to achieve a tamer fall in his fever. I was happy that his immune system was not yet permanently damaged, at least according to Dr. Gerson's theory. But because of the many day-long fevers, he ate less and vomited multiple times. I was less happy about this because he was rapidly losing weight.

I needed to be smarter about performing my secret enemas. Sometimes I accepted that it wasn't going to work. Our longest time without them was a five day break, but by that time, he was getting nervous and listless. I knew that I needed to get the built up toxins out of him as soon as possible.

Because of the hormone pills, his abdomen got distended, and he had flatulence. I massaged and fomented him and put ground cumin into his soups. At night, I put a castor oil pack around his bowels but got so tired that I fell asleep until the evening visitation and got caught. I found myself in an uncomfortable situation. What's more, I didn't really know where I was because of the sudden light in the room. I was saved by the nurse who provided some banal explanation for me, which didn't convince the adjunct at all.

I became more and more apathetic because of the days spent at the hospital. It became hard to stay polite and respectful. I kept fighting but at reduced strength.

On Saturday, the 29th of June, we came in from home for a short ARA-C treatment.

We were temporarily placed into room 5 because Gergő's condition had deteriorated so much that along with his mother and grandmother, his father came in too and was sleeping beside him.

In a calm moment when Nail was watched by another mom, I ran over to them to room 1. He was sitting alone in his railed bed. His parents were smoking their thousandth cigarette a few meters away. It was a cruel experience.

I stepped in and called his name, but he didn't answer. His gaze was fixed on the curtain of the darkened window and beyond it.

There was no trace of fighting, anger, or hate left in him. When his condition worsened, he had to face the reality that he'd be separated from his parents. A few months ago, on his 4th birthday, he was no longer making big plans, didn't finish his drawings, didn't want a fanfare around him, only his family. I watched as he threw out his new toys and went to sleep hugging his old favorite stuffed dog toy.

Now, in this condition of silent acceptance, he made his peace with passing.

I stroked his head with teary eyes, but he didn't even move. I suddenly had the feeling of touching the feathery head of a little pigeon. A soft and warm whiff tickled my hand and felt the embodiment of the ageless spirit as I did so often with Nail. I didn't need words to understand that he was ready to go, maybe waiting for someone to lead him on his way. I didn't want to bother him any longer in this accepting, wise meditation.

That was the last time I saw him in his physical body.

When we came back on Tuesday for the next treatment, the corridor was strangely silent. There was a partial eclipse that night. But not only in the sky.

I didn't need fanfares to realize what had happened.

Death set foot in our room. I was just sitting there and was unable to smile at my son. I was afraid and shivering. But not only me. Others, even members of the staff, were enveloped in silence.

As death unstoppably neared Gergő, I had believed that there would be something that could stop it.

When the mother of little Lilla tiptoed into our room with teary eyes, I asked her almost involuntarily: "I wonder who's next."

"You know, Barbara, I was thinking the same thing."

Was fate listening in?

Following Balázs and Gergő in line, Nail's and Lilla's funerals were on the same day, the 13th of September.

I couldn't process Gergő's passing. For many long weeks, we were living, sleeping, watching TV in the same room, and I unwillingly became a witness to his most intimate moments as well as to his withering. I passed the room feeling frightened as though he were still sitting on that bed. Nobody took his place for days.

I could barely wait to get out of this place. I didn't even care anymore if they closed our CVC at 6 p.m. I needed to get out and as far away as I could.

Spending time at the hospital became torture. Death found its way into my every thought. I attracted any information I previously shooed away like a magnet. I opened the floodgates of the world beyond…

I wanted to know everything about it. How many had passed, in what ways and when…

What happens after death has come.

I tried to focus on Nail's healing and his treatments, trying to avert any future mistakes. My nerves were barely holding out, and I sometimes felt I was no longer sane. Half-consciously, I obtained more and more information about the end, like someone was pouring the inevitable future into my mind through a funnel. There was an ever growing war going on in my soul, yet I still wasn't prepared to take death as my companion.

I wanted to win, no matter the cost. I swept the Morse codes of death under the rug.

On the 2nd of August, we went for an MRI scan to determine the size of the tumor in Nail's ear. According to the medical records, there was "no significant difference in size since May 18th 2000." With the experience I already had, I obtained a copy of the records for ourselves. I didn't bring them back to the hospital until we made photocopies at a nearby place. I wanted to see my son's full records with my own eyes.

That same afternoon, they told us that surgery had become timely. They explained that the bone marrow was finally clean, but the tumor was not reacting to treatments. The cytostatics we injected into his cerebrospinal fluid so many times had somehow not reached their destination. I can still hear the explanation of why we had to wait so long for the surgery if we'd made no progress in months.

"While his system was full of blasts, an operation would have unnecessarily risked complications, stress and damage to his immune system. Now that the marrow is clean, we have remission. Now we have something worth taking the risk for."

According to the latest information, the number of cancerous cells in his bone marrow was down to 2% which is very good. This is only temporary, we can't yet speak about healing, only about the hope that he'll not get worse again.

I couldn't make it to Gergő's funeral, but I probably wouldn't have been able to bear it.

On Wednesday the 9th of August, we were waiting for an intrathecal treatment. I didn't know when they'd call us in. We just waited and waited as we did always when waiting for anesthesia.

The morning came and went, but they still didn't call us. I became more and more angry as time went by. In my thoughts, I'd already called everyone the worst names I could come up with. 2 p.m. 2:30. Still nothing. Never had something like this happened. Nail was crying. He wanted to drink in the pressing heat.

I found our doctor and inquired about why we hadn't been called in yet.

"Oh, Nail should have received an intrathecal treatment today? Let me look at the protocol. You're right. We completely forgot about it… I'll arrange it right now so he can get it tomorrow. Don't worry. A one-day delay won't make a difference."

I didn't even have the strength to answer, not that there was any point. At least I could cry in peace.

Nail lost 0.4 kgs (.088 lbs.). For him this was quite a substantial loss because he was holding stable at 11 kgs (24.25 lbs.) for half a year now. After reaching remission, I decided that a strict diet was no longer necessary, so I added goat milk to his diet. I was actively swathing the area behind his ear. Laci not only gave me instructions but also a few ingredients too. I was hoping that if we could reduce the size of the tumor before the next MRI scan, they may postpone the operation.

The biggest obstacle was that by now we were spending many of our nights at the hospital receiving treatments, so I couldn't do anything without being noticed. I couldn't do it publicly.

On August 10th, the adjunct – who had come back from her summer holiday and was managing the department alone because now the professor was on holiday – asked for a neurological consultation to arrange the operation. According to the neurosurgeon, the tumor showed slow but unmistakable growth and had to be removed because if it spread to vital nerves, it could cause suffocation.

They jointly informed us about the risks of the operation. I also received it in writing after Nail's death.[25]

Of course, it didn't sound like that in real life. Then we had understood that blood would be dripping all through the operation as a precaution precisely because a certain amount of blood loss was expected.

---

[25]. The riskiest complication of the operation is acute bleeding due to the location and hemophiliac nature of the tumor. We intend to perform the operation after finishing and suspending the current chemotherapy block. It will be performed when peripheric blood tests suggest the best opportunity, with transfusion, vvt and thrombocyte transfusion on standby should they be needed.

August 15th was my birthday. It was the thirtieth family birthday this year – except for Nailka, we were all born during summer. Under other circumstances, we would be preparing together. Now that Nail was in such bad condition, we decided to postpone any family celebrations. I was positively surprised: my co-workers gave me champagne, and Laci and Gyöngyi brought me their homemade walnut cake just like they did last week on Ruslan's birthday. It felt really nice. We ate the cake and gifted the champagne to the nurse, who'd told us it was her birthday too. We were not in the mood for toasts anyway…

On August 19th, they finished up chemo treatments so Nail's immune system could regenerate before the operation. We could spend the remaining days at home, only having to go in for blood tests and canola treatments every other day.

On the 28th, they sent us to a heart specialist for an EKG and ultrasound. I asked for a copy of the results, which said: "No abnormal cardiac differences detected."

Two days later, we had another MRI scan to provide the doctors with the latest information.

Among others the report contained the following: "Compared to the results of 12th August 2000 the tumor possibly shows minimal regression as the pressure on the cerebellar hemisphere has slightly decreased."

I hoped this meant good news for everybody.

We brought the results back to the adjunct, and afterward we could go home. They asked us to phone in to get the exact time of the operation.

I already covered the early-September mix-up in the previous chapter. As last words, I would like to share with you the final report written about Nail by our professor on the 5th of September. I first read these words in November 2000 after finding it among the documents we received after our attorney filed our requests.

"NAIL HASZJANOV
09.05.2000.

During the course of the last marrow tests in the aspiratum with flow cytometry the ratio of blast cells was low, but through the biopsied matter analysis focal blasts were detected therefore the remission is only partial. The tumor destroying the skull bone intracranially extending toward the cerebellum located in the right tympanum shows no change after chemotherapy; rather it has slightly progressed according to the MRI scan. Due to the ineffectiveness of chemotherapy, we find the surgical removal of the tumor necessary.

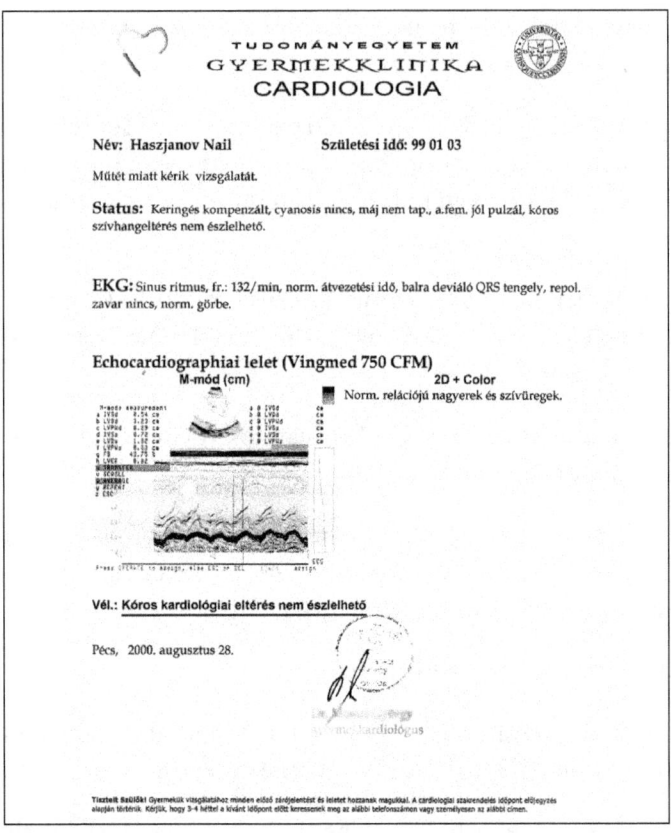

"The substantial reduction of the tumor mass will hopefully make cytostatic treatment more effective. Neurosurgery has been consulted. According to yesterday's opinion, the tumor can be removed in cooperation with otolaryngologists. Professor XY has reviewed the MRI scans and has examined the child. He will perform the operation in XY hospital with the assistance of XY neurosurgeon adjunct. He can't undertake the full removal but will be able to remove a substantial amount of mass. As the intracranial tumor in the middle ear has not changed after treatment, we consider this especially important. Nail's general condition is good. He has no fever, no signs point to an infection. His blood tests are in order, HTC: 30%, fvs: 4500, thr: above

200,000/mm3, abs. granulocyte-count good. In physical status: above lung/ heart abnormalities not heard, the abdomen is soft, well palpated. Liver: 1.5cm, spleen: not palpable. Throat kp. blooded.

Patient has regenerated after last treatment; additional treatment postponed to allow operation. It should be performed as soon as possible because the delay in treatment increases risk of marrow progression and the delay of operation may cause progress of the intracranial tumor. After consulting with Professor XY and adjunct XY, Professor XY has consented to perform the operation on Wednesday. We asked the blood bank for the finding and storage of two units of blood for the operation. We redirected the child to XY hospital on this afternoon.

XY"

Chapter 6

THE TINY WHITE COFFIN

I don't remember how I reached the exit. I just followed the blurred shadow of my husband. I didn't feel the pavement under my feet. I didn't perceive the bustle of people passing by. All I could hear was a medley of sounds that reached me from all directions. My senses stopped working. I felt I'd entered another dimension far from the reality of this world.

A piece of me died with him to follow his steps up there. I became a shadow of myself.

We somehow reached the taxicab stand, and one of the drivers asked: "What's up with the boy?"

"He died," I said in a distant shallow voice. I could barely hear their consoling answer.

"I'm sorry for your loss. My most sincere condolences…"

I nodded my head, and we got in the car. I told him the address, and we were sitting in silence. I didn't dare to look at my husband.

I called the three most important people: my mom, my aunt, and my Italian friend, Antonella.

"It's over. We are at home." I couldn't say more.

In the meantime, my father arrived. He traveled hundreds of kilometers in order to be here with us during the operation. Ruslan looked at him.

"You're late, Dodi. He's gone…" he said in a choked voice.

In no time, we were surrounded by people who cared about us. My mom, Ruslan's Russian friends, and Oleg. He avoided eye contact with me just like I did with everyone else.

I wanted to be alone just to go crazy.

My consciousness was rolling back on the strange road of evolution heading toward my long-lost childhood. I was falling through a door into the deep void where there was nothing. I found myself in a place where nothing made sense.

Tears, tears, tears…

Everywhere. My heart was crying, and I couldn't stop it. I was searching for some kind of meaning or explanation, but my consciousness was captured by the void.

My mum brought me some sedative pills. I thought it would be best to take all of them at once. That would be the only solution for my pain. It didn't make sense to take one, then another one, and so on…

Nail had disappeared from this physical existence, and no drug could bring him back to me. He would be the only drug that could resurrect the dying mother inside my body.

I let this painful shadow overwhelm my existence. It came uninvited, grabbed me and pulled me down to the highway of deepest emotions of another world. My soul got home. I left my body behind somewhere I can't even remember.

I went to the kindergarten for Csingiz. My mom wanted to come with me, but I had to do it alone. It was my job.

The children were playing outside. The air was full of joy and laughter. I was just standing there in black and could barely see Csingiz through the tears.

I went to him, took his hand, and I said: "Csingiz. Come with me. I have to tell you something sad but very important. I'm going to be honest with you because we always tell each other the truth, right? After the operation today, Nailka has gone. He left behind his tired body so that he can take a rest now. Before he left, he said that he wants you to know that he will always love you. You know, you were the most important person for him. He will never leave you. You don't have to be afraid. He said that if you want to see him again, you just have to close your eyes. He is your guardian angel now."

"Why did he go there, Mom? I don't want him to go there, and I don't want to close my eyes. I want him to come back," Csingiz said, crying.

"Don't cry, my darling. Mommy is not crying, you see?" I answered with a smile. "He will come back to us. But he has to find another body. A healthier one."

"But we have to wait for so long. Who will I play with?"

The immense sadness affected Csingiz as well. He was just sitting in the corner without a word. Ruslan was maddened with anger. He kept saying: "They killed him. Do you understand? They killed our son. They didn't give him blood. They left him bleeding to death. My mother will go mad."

He cried, cried, cried. He grabbed Nailka's pram and high chair and put them in the garage. He couldn't stand the sight of his son's belongings. I didn't even try to calm him down. I hoped that his mother would be able to stop him from a total breakdown before he hurt himself.

I needed to behave myself and focus on my other son, Csingiz. I tried to stay calm. I encouraged him to draw pictures of the things that Nailka loved.

"We will send it to him via angel mail," I said. "We put it into the mailbox, and by the time you wake tomorrow, the letter will be taken by him."

We started drawing together. Smiling grapes, tomatoes, cherries. Curvy croissants, salami, and potatoes. The neighbor's dog, Lisa, and the small kitten that we made drink milk the day before yesterday. We drew a motorcycle, the yellow jeep, a spotted ball and horse chestnut.

"This is it, Mom. I can't think of anything else," said Csingiz thoughtfully.

"Mom," he continued. "How will he take the letter out of the mailbox? He's not tall enough."

"Oh, don't worry about it," I answered. "Angels have wings and can fly. They can fly anywhere."

I don't remember the time when our guest left. The next thing I realized was the silence. My husband and his father were sitting outside the garden. They were drinking wine and smoking cigarettes.

I made a bed for Csingiz and me in the living room. I couldn't bear to sleep in the double bed that the three of us used last night. When I looked at

Nail's bedclothes and pajamas, I felt a sudden sharp stab in my stomach. I cried out in pain. I collapsed on the ground, and I pushed my hands against my abdomen. I desperately tried to find a better position, but nothing eased the feeling that was very similar to labor pain. I thought this is the end. I cried, and I didn't know why.

The absence of my son was unbearable, and every piece of my body was longing for him. I opened my arms and held the emptiness. Thinking that I heard his voice, I roamed the house trying to find him. I was scraping the wall and crying in pain, and I inhaled his scent lingering around his clothes.

Csingiz was asleep, and I was just sitting in the armchair next to the phone. I was waiting for a call from the professor who would say, "You won't believe what happened. This is a miracle. Nail came alive on the dissection table, so you can come and take his home."

Just when I thought I couldn't bear the pain anymore, the physical pain disappeared. I knew that I gave birth to Nail's aura, and he was ready to leave my body alone.

On the next day, on September 7th, Ruslan and my father went to take over the documents and Nail's clothes. When they arrived back home, Ruslan handed me a plastic bag with our son's shirt and trousers, the case of his CVC, a piece of cloth and a picture of the Virgin Mary in it. I embraced it tightly as if I were waiting for those to come alive.

"They didn't even know whether he was a boy or a girl. They said, here are the belongings of your daughter. It doesn't matter to them…" he waved his hand sadly.

We received a bunch of mourning telegrams. It felt good knowing that people were thinking of my child.

My next task was to gather enough strength to organize the last journey of my son. I had to buy some black clothes and shoes. I never liked this color. I contacted a local funeral agency. My mom accompanied me everywhere, and it meant a lot to me. We'd never been this close to each other.

It was shocking to step inside a room full of coffins and funeral supplies. As I was sitting there, I realized that I was just a few hundred meters away from the clinic where the doctors wished me luck a couple of days ago.

The memory moved me, and I had to stand up. I looked around, and I was horrified by the coffins in different sizes. I burst into tears.

I wasn't ready to accept Nail's death.

They showed me two child-sized coffins, and I had to pick the one that was the right size for Nail. I wanted a plain white coffin without ornaments. Nail's pall was also prepared to size.

"Shall we leave the child coffins up here?" asked the employee. "Or should I put them back in the basement?"

"Yes, take them back," said the boss. "They don't need to be here. We're not showing off child coffins. Sorry… Where were we?"

We chose white rose for the wreaths, paid for the administration, the wooden grave marker, the transport, the dressing, the grave, the grave-digging and many other service fees.

"I talked with the pathology," said the boss, breaking the silence. "Guess what! They won't ask any money for cooling the body. It would be 4000 forints per day, but he is so small that they can put him beside someone."

I was unable to say thank you for such a "moving" gesture. I turned away and began to cry.

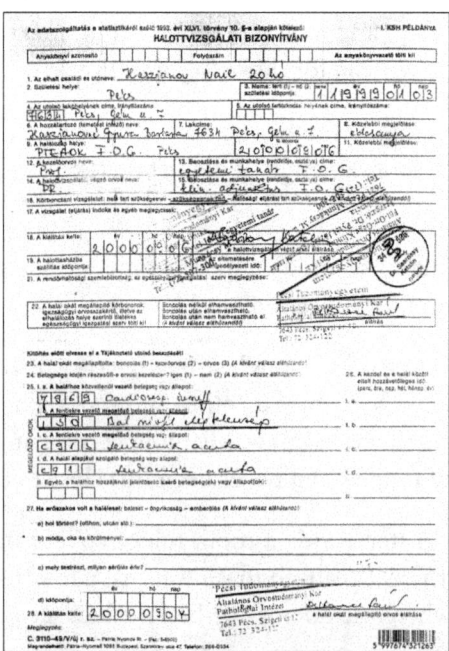

We agreed to meet the next day and bring some clothes for Nail and a few toys that we would like to bury with him. In the meantime, they obtained the death certificate.

"And don't forget the envelope," they shouted as we were heading back to the car. "They used to give 5000 forints for dressing up the deceased."

As agreed, we brought his clothes, a little yellow duck toy, a hooting ambulance car – just like the one I was waiting for on the day he died – and my mobile phone. I asked them to put it in his hand as a symbol. I didn't need it anymore, but Nail loved it. I gave it to him, and I wanted him to know that we would stay in touch forever.

I handed over the envelope with the money and asked them to cut a tiny lock of hair and a bit of his fingernail. Probably I wouldn't be able to do this.

Then we moved on to the discussion of the ceremony.

Nail's death caused huge chaos in my life, including my faith in God. I didn't know what truth was. I was angry with God. I was angry with Jesus, and I was angry with the Virgin Mary as well. They fooled me into believing in miracles.

"Why him?" I asked the heavens. "Why do you call yourself God if you are unable to save a child? You haven't done anything to stop this madness. These children suffer more in this hell on Earth than Jesus. Why don't you let them heal? Don't you have a heart? What has Nail done to you?" I was left without an answer.

I didn't want a priest. I didn't want a proverb. I wanted to avoid clichés because my son deserved more than an ordinary funeral.

I heard that Gergő's funeral six weeks ago was a touching and intimate American style funeral. When Nail was still with us, I always thought that the ceremony doesn't matter after our loved one had passed away. Now I realized how important it was actually.

I wanted to find a resting place for my son as soon as possible far away from the sterile harshness of this world. I chose the American style funeral, which is becoming more and more popular – mainly among child funerals – in Hungary. In this city, it was a completely new thing. I informed the funeral agency that I was going to collect all the necessary information about this type of funeral.

The protocol of the ceremony is very similar to the usual one. The difference is that after the ceremony in the funeral parlor, they placed the coffin in the yard on a so-called St. Michael's horse, which is actually two trestles. Here the grieving crowd says goodbye to the deceased and everyone leaves. The coffin is placed into the grave, and they cover it with soil and arrange the flowers on the top. Thirty minutes later, the close relatives return to the grave for a final goodbye.

We agreed on the ceremony with the funeral agent. Now I had to pick the appropriate music. There was a man who was in charge of this task. I arranged a meeting with him because I wanted to make clear a few things before the funeral.

We were waiting for him in the office, my mother, Ruslan, and I.

"Hello, condolences," he said entering the room vigorously. I was shocked by this greeting. Ruslan started talking about Nail. Later, I joined the conversation and tried to convince him to forget about everything and start seeing the world through the eyes of a twenty-month-old child. Nail meant the world to us.

He pulled out a paper from his pocket with an empty table on it. It said: the name of the relatives, their classification and so on. I told him to forget about this terrible official procedure because I didn't want to hear about it. He was offended. He pulled out a bunch of pre-written texts and said: "Excuse me, ma'am. As an experienced professional, I know exactly what a funeral looks like. Look at this one." And he handed over an awful stereotyped text.

I couldn't read the whole page. It was terrible because it was missing the most important aspects of our connection with Nail. I asked him to use the words "Mom" and "Dad" instead of "Mother" and "Father" but he was not willing to. We disagreed on almost all aspects of the text. He said he didn't want to use colloquial terms.

"Wait a minute. This is all about my son, right? I pay you eight thousand forints for a fifteen minute long speech, but you will read out what I order you. Forget about these awful texts."

"Okay."

We agreed on this. As we were walking away, they handed over the autopsy report. The upper half of the paper was full of data. Below, there was a note about the reason of death. I was astounded since it said: *cardio-resp. insuff., left heart failure, leukaemia acuta.*

I couldn't believe my eyes. They performed an operation on my son, they put a cover on an open wound, they left him unattended for minutes, they made us watch him bleed to death, and after all of these, they state that the reason of his death was "left heart failure." I was disgusted.

I ran out to the street heading to the clinic, which was just a few hundred meters away from the office. My husband followed me.

We entered at the back door and stopped in front of our head doctor's door. She answered our knocking, and I put the autopsy report in her face.

"Why are you lying? My son bled to death."

"I'm very sorry, Barbara," she replied. "But I wasn't there at the time of Nail's operation. I'm not authorized to take sides."

"Yes, I know. But you've probably heard what happened."

"Yes. You called me. So did my colleagues. I don't know what to say. It's horrible."

"If you had been here, Nail would be still alive. You know that. You've promised me that there would be enough blood."

"You shouldn't say such things, Barbara."

"Look at him," I showed her some old pictures. "He used to be healthy when these photos were taken. Look at him. A beautiful, fair-haired little boy. And what do we have now? He was the corner of our heart, the light of our eyes, the single most important person for us. I would dress even my heart to black."

"You scare me, Barbara. You have a son, Csingiz. It must be very hard for him, too."

"I can't stand this whole thing any longer. I can't. I just want to have my child back somehow…"

Feeling completely broken down, I was waiting for my mother to buy some cassettes with the necessary music for the funeral. As an ambulance and a blood transport car were passing by, I thought they won't be late this time…

I was standing in the middle of a huge music store and didn't know what to choose. When I asked the salesman to help me pick some music for the funeral of a child, he became embarrassed and couldn't help. I needed to put together ten minutes of music.

At home, I threw the cassettes into the corner and couldn't even think about the funeral.

I called Gergő's mother and grandmother to ask for some help with the music. They were surprised to hear about my hardships as the notary of their town had arranged everything: she picked the music, decorated the room and prepared a beautiful ceremony. It was heartfelt and personal, they said. I asked them if they could show me the text to draw inspiration from it.

I'm thankful for everything. Not only for sharing this intimate text with me but also for the obituary and for all their other suggestions.

"We brought pine branches to the grave," they said. "We asked the men to place them on the top of the coffin before covering it with soil. And you should take a few sedative pills before the funeral. Believe me: that will be the most horrific hour."

As I opened the letter, my memories about Gergő kept rushing back. There was a quote at the end from Exupéry's *The Little Prince*. It was just perfect.

I'd been working on the farewell for two days. I knew that I couldn't go back with this text to that man at the funeral agency. I didn't want to, for that matter. But what should I do then?

One of my friends suggested asking an actor for the job. I liked the idea, and I had nothing to lose. I opened the phone book and looked up the number of the actor who had been organizing performances for children throughout the city's schools.

I dialed the number, but I could barely talk. Finally, I pulled myself together and told him that the text was ready, but I was in need of someone who could read it out loud at the funeral. He said that it would be too painful for him but promised to help.

It was Sunday, and I had just a few days until Wednesday…

I got a call in the afternoon. I heard the voice of Gergő's mother on the other side: "I need to tell you that… that… Lilla passed away."

I'd already been living in an unbearable state of mind, and this was enough! I couldn't believe it. I started screaming and shouting. This can't be happening!

We just met two days ago.

We hadn't even told her that Nail died. We didn't want to upset her… She was not over the loss of her little friend, Gergő.

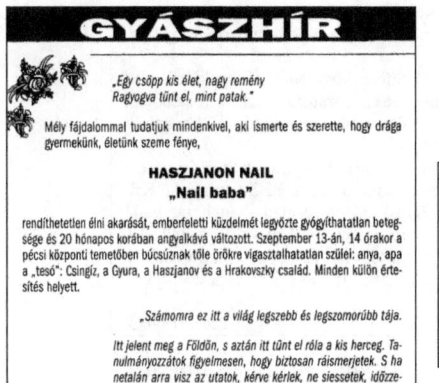

Nail's obituaries

We met the young actor at the buffet of the theater on Monday, and he agreed to read out the farewell text. He was the first to read my work. He was reading through the text silently. After he finished, I asked him whether it was too pathetic. He shook his head. I showed him a few photos of Nail and told him about the most important steps of our journey. When we shook hands at the end, I knew that he was the right person for this role. He was worthy of this mission.

Using my limited skills, I put together the music during the night. I used three cassettes because the music would be played three times during the funeral, and I wanted to make sure that everything would be played in the correct order.

KÖSZÖNET

„Ne állj zokogva síromnál;
Nem vagyok ott.
Nem alszom.
De ott vagyok az ezer szélben, mi fú.
Én vagyok a gyémánt csillogás a havon.
Én vagyok a napfény az érett gabonán.
Én vagyok a szelíd őszi eső.
Amikor felébreszt a reggeli zsivaj,
Ott vagyok minden hangban veled,
A csendesen köröző madár szavában, de én
Vagyok a csillag is, mely rád süt az éjszakában.
Ne állj hát zokogva síromnál;
Nem vagyok ott.
Nem haltam meg."
ISMERETLEN

Hálás szívvel, őszintén mondunk köszönetet mindazoknak, akik eljöttek a kicsi **HASZJANOV NAÍL** temetésére, és fájdalmunkon enyhíteni szerettek volna.
Köszönet a rengeteg - névtelenül is küldött - koszorúért, virágok özönéért, táviratokért, valamennyi rokonunknak, barátunknak, kollégánknak, szomszédainknak, ismerőseinknek. Köszönjük a megható búcsúbeszédet Széll Horváth Lajos színésznek.
Tiszteletteljes részvétükért külön köszönetet mondunk a Ráczvárosi Óvodának és a „Barna" csoportos szülőknek, a PBS Hungária Kft. dolgozóinak, a MATÁV PONT dolgozóinak és a család ottani barátainak, a Magyar Külker Bank Rt. dolgozóinak, az 1989-ben a Lőwey Klára Gimnáziumban érettségizett IV. C osztálynak és osztályfőnöküknek, a pékség dolgozóinak, orosz barátainknak, fodrász néninknek, ügyvéd barátunknak és „Zé"nővérnek.

A gyászoló család

Acknowledgements of participants in Nail's funeral

Fate was kind to me that day. I entered Nail's room in search of an old cassette of The Little Prince. It was a musical version of the book, but we'd never opened the box. I found it, and I put in into the cassette player. I fast-forwarded to the last song entitled "Farewell." I pressed the play button, and that minute, I knew that I'd found the perfect music for Nail's farewell.

In the evening, I asked Csingiz whether he wanted to come to his brother's funeral. He said yes. I completely understood his decision. He wanted to say goodbye to Nail, and this was going to be time. The only and unrepeatable opportunity. A lot of people tried to dissuade me from this idea, but I believed that Csingiz had the right to decide. I thought that shutting Csingiz out would make him feel alone and would convey the idea that death and grief are too horrible to be faced. I wanted to give him the opportunity to experience his beloved brother's death in a simple, honest, straightforward and non-threatening way. He even had a surprising wish.

"Mom, I'd really love to see him again before they close the coffin. I want to see his body which he left behind."

"I don't think it's a good idea, darling," I replied.

"But I want to see him. He left so quickly that we didn't even have time to say goodbye to each other," he said, sobbing.

Ruslan and I decided that we would go and see Nail's body and decide whether the coffin would be closed or open during the ceremony.

We got an appointment for Tuesday morning at 7 o'clock. There was a building standing behind the main cemetery. It looked exactly the same as the surrounding buildings. The sign above the entrance said, "Funeral warehouse."

I crossed the dewy cemetery shaking from the cold. Ruslan and my father were following my footsteps in silence. A thick layer of fog was covering the ground. We could barely see the mossy headstones.

We met my mother at the entrance of the warehouse. She was wearing black, and her eyes were red from crying.

"I saw the car. They've just arrived with Nail. I told them I'll wait for you," she said.

We entered the hangar-like building.

I noticed my son's dazzling white coffin instantly. It was placed on a shabby table. A shroud was covering Nail's entire body. The temporary catafalque was right in front of the cold storage. Mist was swirling through the gap of the door, giving the whole scenario an eerie mood.

My body was freezing, especially my heart. As we slowly approached the coffin, I felt unbearable coldness coming from inside me. No one moved.

I knew I had to do it. I took a deep breath and lifted the shroud. My husband ran out of the building instantly, and I stepped back as well screaming in horror. I was sure that it was not my son lying there. It couldn't be him. But then where was he? Where was Nail? Was he alive?

My mom burst into tears, and my father was crying too. I slowly realized that this tiny lifeless body in front of me used to be Nail's body once. I was shaking as I touched his arms, which were crossed over his chest. At least his hands were still recognizable.

No words can express how horrible the sight was. I can't find any appropriate adjectives.

His eyes were open wide and stared straight into the distance through his lightless pupils. I could see clotted blood on his little white teeth indicating that he was fighting until his last breath. There were dark red spots under his lips, but the worst was still to come…

There was a long cut on his scalp from one ear to the other. Like he was cut in half. The wound was closed with hasty stitches, and the around the forehead, there was a red rigid rectangle shaped plate covering the cavity.

I didn't want to look at his face. Therefore, I lifted the shroud and touched his clothes. His shirt was not in place, but I didn't have the strength to move it and see the cuts on his chest, stomach, and heart. I quickly adjusted his clothes and buttoned the shirt. There were the little duck and the ambulance car lying beside his body. In the next moment, I realized that something was missing. I couldn't find the mobile phone. This was too much for me.

I ran into the office shouting where two men were eating their breakfast among dozens of urns.

"Where is the phone?" I shouted.

"What phone? We haven't seen any phone."

"Look, I put the phone in a bed next to the toys and told your boss that I want the phone to be placed in my son's hand. This is very important for us. I told her that I'm going to check it. But now can't see it anywhere."

"The thing is that we haven't even received the phone. We only got the toys."

"Listen to me carefully. The funeral is tomorrow. I'm a journalist with more than enough things to say about the death of my son to the public. If you don't go and find the phone now, I swear that I'll call the representatives of all the written and electronic media here and tell the whole country that your company steals from dead infants… Do you still think it is worth it to steal that goddamn phone?"

"Wait, ma'am. You need to calm down. We totally understand that you're in an extremely troubled state of mind, but we don't know anything about this phone. Let me call my boss. She'll fix everything, I'm sure."

I went back to Nail, crying. I looked at his wooden grave marker and discovered several spelling mistakes right away. I told the men to correct at least the accented characters on the grave marker and on the side of the coffin by tomorrow. But I was so nervous that I didn't really care.

Five minutes later, the man came to us and said that they had found the missing phone.

"It is still at the pathology. It must have fallen out of the bag, and they didn't know whose it was."

"You could've come up with a better story."

"They will bring it here tomorrow and…"

"No!" I interrupted him. "I want to have it right now. I'll take it to my son's hand. When can I have it?"

"It will be in our office by 10 o'clock."

"Great. Could you do me a favor?"

"Yes, of course. What is it?"

"Close the eye of my son, please."

"I'm afraid that won't be possible."

"Why not?"

"Because the eyelids don't work after death."

We went outside the building, and I opened the newspaper. I turned the page to the obituaries. It was there – but they made a mistake. The family name of my son was spelled incorrectly. I became upset.

I dialed the publisher who was my ex-boss. I told him what happened. He really felt bad about it and expressed his condolences.

We also got our phone back.

"I apologize, Barbara," she said. "The pathologist gave it back to me. I thought it wasn't real."

"Yeah, they probably realized it…"

"This is horrible. I'm very sorry."

"You know, if I had turned out tomorrow, I don't know how I would've reacted."

"There's one more thing. Nothing really important but…"

"What?"

"You son won't be buried in the first row but the second. Believe me, it's even better because tombs get mossy under the trees, but Nail's grave isn't going to be surrounded by tall trees. The proposed place is on the spot that looks like an open plane meadow."

"No. I won't accept it. This is enough. You promised me that Nail would be buried in the first row…"

"You know what? I'll take you to the cemetery right now, and you can talk about this issue with them."

We got into the car, and I told her the whole story about what happened in the morning.

"In the Western countries, this is not how it works. Proper body painting, makeup, a tasteful room where we can present the deceased to the relatives – we do everything to catch up with them, but it's not easy."

We waited for her in the car. After a few minutes, she returned with great news: our son would be buried in the first row. This is ridiculous. Parents have to fight even for their child's grave.

On September 13th, we got up very early, although we hadn't slept much during the night. I didn't know what to expect from the ceremony which was to begin at 2 p.m. Time slowed down to a snail's pace, and we spent the morning in silence. I couldn't think of anything else but Nail.

Holding his little clothes, I was praying to him to give me enough strength and not to leave me alone during the most difficult moments of my life.

I began to feel numbness and slowly lost control of my body. We were approaching the cemetery. I was holding an enlarged black and white photo of Nail. Ruslan wanted to have the photo for himself, but I couldn't let it out of my hands. Csingiz was walking beside me. I was sweating.

Finally, we got there. I remember people standing in front of the cemetery gate. One of my mother's colleagues was carrying an enormous wreath. This made me realize that I was going to bury my child today.

I felt the earth move under my feet, and everything blurred behind the black veil of my perplexed mind. I couldn't perceive anything or anybody. I observed my body from outside, and it seemed completely strange. I wasn't me.

I left Csingiz with my mom. Ruslan and I went upstairs to say goodbye to Nail. A lady was waiting for us in front of the room. I instructed her not to open the door for anybody.

Before we entered the room, she touched my arm and said: "Excuse me, ma'am. I'm afraid we have some bad news. I know that we promised to close his eyes before the ceremony, but we couldn't do it. I'm sorry. Please be prepared for the sight."

"I understand. Thank you."

The room was a bit dim. The coffin was standing at the other end of the room, close to the side door. In front of the coffin, there was a myriad of flowers lying on the floor. My father and Ruslan were already there. The door closed behind me, but I was unable to move forward. I knew exactly what was waiting for me.

I lay my eyes on the wreaths and flowers. They touched my soul. I could feel the love and honor of all those people who had been thinking of us. This gave me strength.

I tiptoed toward the coffin as if I didn't want to wake him up. Tears were rolling down on my face, and I had to stop to take a handkerchief.

I'd never felt anything like this before. It wasn't my son. It was a stranger lying in that coffin. I forced myself to touch the ice cold hands. It didn't even resemble my son. I wasn't sure whether all of these were real or I was in a dream.

I stepped back and opened my handbag. I started searching for the phone. I was searching through the contents of the bag. I couldn't find it anywhere. My stuff started falling out of my bag. I was panicking.

The lady who was guarding the room stepped inside, and I ran at her with Nail's photo in my hand.

"Look at him. Look at him. It's he beautiful? Like an angel," I explained. "The child who is lying in that coffin is not him. That's a different person."

I don't know why I was doing this. Probably she had met even worse cases during her work. She'd seen everything imaginable: the lifeless bodies, the horrible faces, the plastic stiffness. Nail was just another case for her, nothing special.

"Yes, he must have been a cute child," she answered, looking at the photo.

I continued searching for the phone and finally managed to find it at the bottom of my bag. I went to the coffin and put the phone in Nail's hand.

I've never been asthmatic, but in that moment, I felt I couldn't breathe. It was scary. I was choking, and I ceased to perceive the world around me.

She came to me and put her hand on my shoulder.

"You need to calm down," she said, a little frightened. "I suggest that we close the coffin."

She accompanied me to the ceremonial hall through the side door. She kept talking to me to make sure that I was fine. I asked her about the place of the coffin, that of the microphone and Nail's enlarged photo, and something about the flowers. She managed to take my attention off the horrible part of this experience. I calmed down a bit.

We went back to the room. I nodded my head, and they closed the coffin.

I could see Csingiz through the little window of the door. I went outside and held his hand.

The crowd was gathering in front of the door of the ceremonial hall. According to the plans, we would've had half an hour to say goodbye to Nail, but it was too much.

As I was standing there, I could feel my soul leaving my body again. I can't remember the exact details of the next minutes. Maybe there was the GP of my children with his assistant, the young actor and lots of other faces. I remember someone opening the door. I could hear Ruslan's voice in my ear saying that we had to stay strong because it would be the hardest part of this craziness.

"Just consider that the body lying there is not Nail's. His soul has left. He's somewhere else now. In a happier place," whispered Ruslan.

Csingiz was standing between us. He kept looking up at his father and me. I placed Nail's photo in front of the coffin, and Csingiz put a small blue car next to it.

Originally, we wanted to bring his favorite red car, but that one disappeared a few days ago. Therefore, Csingiz picked another one. A week later, we found the red car behind his bed. We developed some posthumous film rolls about Nailka's last days, and in one of them, he was standing there in his pajamas holding the blue car.

The ceremony started with the melody of *The Little Prince*: "There was just a yellow flash close to his ankle. He remained a moment without moving. He didn't yell. That didn't even make a noise because of the sand…"

The actor read the speech. I knew every word by heart. A hurricane must have picked me up and carried me away somewhere so I could be with Nail. I entered into a different dimension.

I saw my body lying down there. It was empty. In that moment, I realized that death doesn't exist. It is just an illusion. We are much more than our physical existence. Someone or something else was controlling my movements. Death is nothing but a metamorphosis. I can say at that moment, I was not alive. Probably this is why I can't remember the details.

We were walking toward the grave. There was a young man in front of us, carrying Nail's wooden grave marker. I moved like a marionette. I could hear the music from the background: "Mom" (by *Emberek*), "I Go Away" (by *Péter Máté*), "Requiem" (by *Karthagó*) and "Farewell" (by *Edda*).

We stopped next to the grave, and the young actor recited the closing lines of *The Little Prince*. It was followed by the condolences, and this was the hardest part of the ceremony. I had to realize that we are the protagonists of this whole story – we are the ones who stay behind. Nail's death is our tragedy.

The crowd scattered. Csingiz started pulling my arm, crying. He must have been scared because he saw me crying during the condolences. He was completely exhausted. We left the cemetery and waited for the men at my mother's place, just five minutes from the cemetery.

Ruslan and his friends decided to stay and wait for the coffin to be lowered into the grave. He didn't want to leave his son alone in those moments.

Nail was never born and never died. He only visited this planet Earth between January 3, 1999 from 1:50 p.m. and September 6, 2000 1:50 p.m.

I completely understood his decision. According to Muslim belief, this is what he had to do.

An hour later, we returned to the cemetery. The grave was covered by flowers and wreaths. Everything was peaceful. Rays of sunshine were filtering through the branches of the trees, illuminating the final resting place of my beloved son.

Chapter 7
THE SLOW AWAKENING

I thought that everything would be easier after the funeral. I was wrong.

The madness had just begun.

I couldn't even get out of bed for a while. I cried a lot silently in a crazy trance. I was vegetating between life and death.

I had to put myself together from time to time just for the sake of my other son, Csingiz. It was extremely hard for him to tolerate my overwhelming depression. Even though I believed in eternal life, the lack of Nail's physical existence caused unbearable pain. I felt I was going mad.

I often woke up with a start at night, sweating. I seemed to hear his voice crying "Mom, Mom, Mom!" or to feel his little body lying between Csingiz and me, holding our hands as always. I turned to hug him, but there was just an empty space, a tremendous gap between Csingiz and me. We kept his space between us for a long time: none of us wanted to "overlie" his body.

I didn't want to talk to anybody. All vital instincts disappeared from my tortured body. I couldn't smell; the vibrant colors hurt my eyes, and I was disturbed by crowds. I was falling into a deep ocean of darkness.

After the death of Nail, we put everything out of sight that made us remember his loss: the pram, the high chair, the baby bottle, his toys and his little clothes. We put everything up in the attic and in the garage.

I didn't want to throw those things away. I just wanted to distance myself from the memories. In my imagination, I had to relive his death and his funeral over and over again.

Ruslan was also suffering in silence. Instead of us joining forces, we isolated ourselves from each other. We tried to swim against the current on our own.

It took me a week to collect my strength and visit my son's grave. I was afraid of my reaction. Then I plucked up my courage, and from that time on, I went out to the cemetery twice or even three times a day. Wind and rain didn't matter for me. I was searching for him. I twiddled with the falling leaves for long hours. I watched the crows flying by and talked to the blackbird that landed on the wooden grave marker. When I got tired, I sat on a heap of bricks. When silence hurt my ears, I started talking to the photo of Nail that was still hanging on the grave. I visited all the little graves of the children's parcel and greeted them. I knew that I was almost going completely mad and transforming into a creepy lunatic roaming among the graves.

I used to return home late in the afternoons when Csingiz arrived from the kindergarten. I neglected him.

A thin layer of dust was covering the picture books and the toys in Csingiz's room. He begged me to read out his favorite stories, but I kept postponing it. Csingiz locked himself into his own world since we failed to behave like real parents.

Our friends told us that it we relied on Csingiz during our tragedy, he would restore our faith in life. But we fled from facing these painful challenges.

Sadness, outbursts, and self-accusations were our daily visitors.

A week after the funeral, a car stopped in front of our house. They were bailiffs, who said that they would start collecting our belonging tomorrow.

We took loans to boost our business, but during the last six months, we had lost everything. Our creditors became impatient; we couldn't pay the taxes. We used loans to pay off other loans. We were unable to make our mortgage payments; therefore, the bank wanted to repossess the house. All this happened because Nail's treatment was extremely expensive, but I didn't care. I would've done anything for my son.

When Nail had been diagnosed with his disease, banks turned away from us. Only a long-term loan could've saved us from disaster. We were on the edge of bankruptcy, and there was no one to help us except a few friends. My Italian friend paid for Nail's funeral, and my ex-classmates collected money for our family. I can't thank them enough. Otherwise, we lived from day to day.

The solitude was unbearable, and now I had to blame myself for the bankruptcy of my family.

Ruslan and I quarreled almost every day. He started drinking and smoking, although he always despised that lifestyle. I started drinking as well, but wine and cigarettes only shook me out of the daze that kept me away from reality. I wasn't taking tranquilizers because I thought that it would only prolong my bereavement.

Csingiz started to behave aggressively in the kindergarten. He was swearing, fighting, and spitting on the other children. Once he even tried to run out of the garden and jump in front of a car. He witnessed our self-destruction at home.

There were times when I begged my husband to let me die so that I could be together with Nail, and then he and Csingiz could go to Moscow and start a new life.

"Believe me; this is the only solution. We'll never be happy again," I kept telling him.

I really felt that something had died inside me forever.

Once I called my mom and told her that I was going away… I had absolutely nothing to live for, no hope, and my life was ruined beyond repair. I begged her to forgive me for jumping off the TV tower. I even wrote a letter of farewell in which I stated that I wanted to be buried next to my son.

My mother jumped into a taxi and came for me. I packed my stuff and moved to her place with Csingiz. My stepfather visited us that afternoon unexpectedly and wanted my mom to pay the purchase price of half of the house that my mother was living in.

I was listening to the quarrel for a while, tearing up old wounds; then I was fed up and left the house, crying. I knew that my mother got into this situation because she wanted to help Nail.

I was heading to the cemetery… It was getting late. The cold crawled under my skin, and the salty tears were stinging my eyes. I remember candlelight dancing all around. I thought it would be best to lie down beside my son. The next morning, they would find my dead, heartbroken body on Nail's grave. I wanted to put an end to my suffering. The next thing I can remember was my mom lifting me up from the ground.

Ruslan spent the next few weeks in Moscow. Finally, he could express his feelings honestly, in his mother tongue. I moved to my mom's with Csingiz. It was the first time that Csingiz didn't want to go home. Actually, he asked me to sell the house and move to another place. He never talked about his brother, but I knew that he was suffering inside. He put away the toys and books that they used to play with together, and he wrapped himself in a significant silence.

When Ruslan returned from Moscow, we moved back together in our old home and continued destroying each other. We had alienated ourselves from our true selves and from each other. We never thought that our son's death would active our most brutal instincts. I packed, and we decided to separate.

We had lost Nail, and we had lost something in our relationship as well. The fruit of our love, the most important person in our life, had died. No one else could take his place. Blaming the whole world around us, we pushed love far from ourselves. We didn't know how to love, and we didn't want to be loved. We thought that by signing the papers before the operation, we had become responsible for the death of our child. We couldn't wash away our sin. I couldn't forgive myself.

Maybe, Ruslan blamed me for Nail's death for a while.

I cried a lot and visited the cemetery every day. We always went separately because we had different mourning patterns, and we didn't want to be involved in each other's pain.

One morning, I was walking along the wall of the cemetery along the children's parcel. I was holding a bunch of white pansies. I always brought white flowers since they represent purity and innocence. As I looked up, I noticed Ruslan at Nail's grave. He was caressing the head marker of our son, crying. I was moved, and I couldn't say a word. At that moment, I realized that Ruslan had the exact same right to be in pain as I did. I went to him. I held his hand, and we hugged each other.

"We need to have him back," he said with tears in his eyes. "This is our only hope."

"We'll get him back, you'll see. God will help us."

For the first time in the last few months, we were together. It wasn't about desire or satisfaction. We made love in silence, and I was praying for Nail's return. When we reached the peak, I know that both of us were thinking of Nail.

I don't know why, but I knew that a new life was conceived inside me.

Then things slowly began to change.

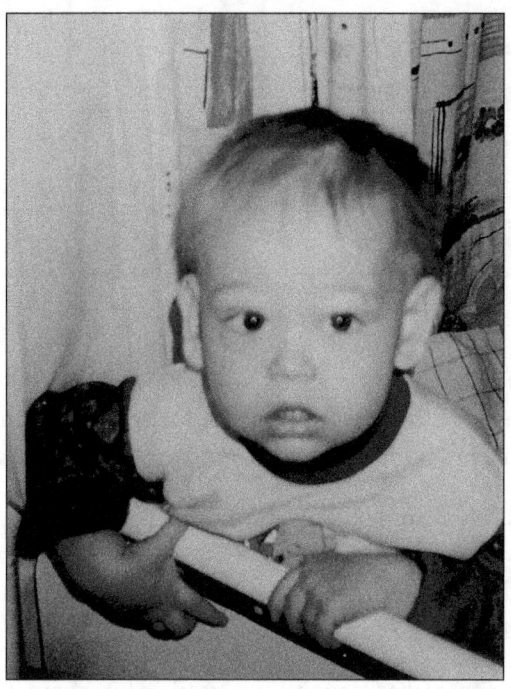

We didn't talk about divorce anymore. We started to spend a lot of time with Csingiz. We paid attention to his mental development. I started to find my old self again, but I experienced ambivalent feelings.

I had a photo of Nail enlarged, and I hung it in front of our bed, next to the one that I used at the funeral. When I wanted to talk to Nail, it was no longer my first thought to run to his grave, but I started communicating with him through this picture.

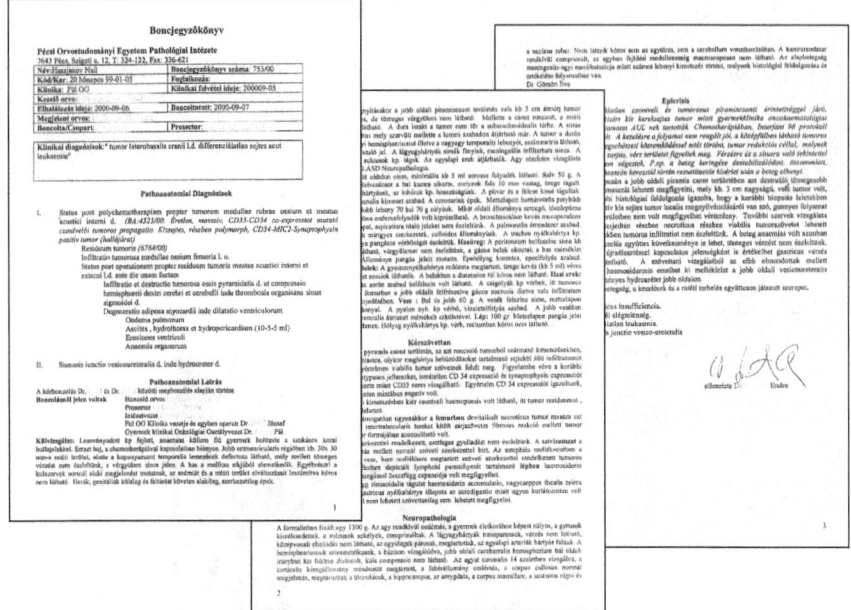

Nail's autopsy report

I made a homemade altar from silk flowers and lit a candle every day. We put photos of Nail in different spots in the house. We were no longer fleeing from the memories, but we were ready to welcome him back.

I wasn't an easy ride. Some things were still impossible for us. For example, watching old videotapes. I pressed the play button twice, but I became very upset, so I hid them at the bottom of the cupboard. Ruslan couldn't even open the photo album.

I started to write a diary again and read a lot about thanatology, the scientific study of death. I wanted to learn about death, about dying. I wanted to understand what Nail might have experienced as he was leaving this world. I sent letters to the pathology and wanted clear answers to my question about that day.

In the meantime, I gave a late night report on TV about the conditions that surround dying people in Hungary. I trumpeted my pain, but I didn't intend to take revenge or file a lawsuit against the doctors. I knew that it wouldn't bring my son back. I even saw sparks of regret in the professor's eyes – though I'm not sure whether it was only a sign of disgrace or if he felt awful about Nail's death.

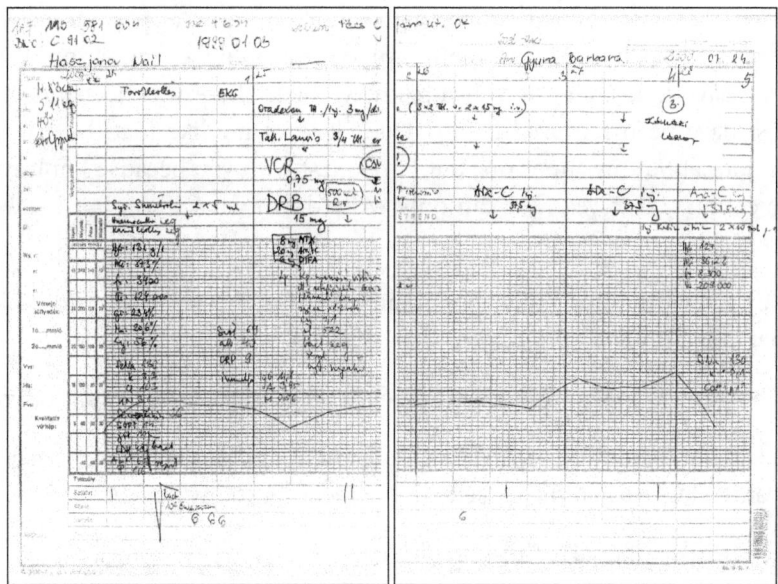

The fact of "remissio" written by the professor himself on Nail's medical chart

On the pathology, they already received us as personae non gratae because of the TV interview. The doctor performing the autopsy immediately had me sign the preliminary autopsy report, saying that he'd been ordered to do so.

"We usually don't ask relatives to do this, but in your case, they made an exception." He excused himself.

I demanded an explanation regarding the cause of death, and I waved Nail's heart ultrasound and EKG results.

"Look, this is from a few days before his death. Everything looked good. So how could he have died from heart failure?" I asked.

"Ultimately everyone dies from that."

"But he bled out right in front of my eyes. Why didn't you write anything about that?"

"Ma'am, I didn't find any evidence of external bleeding. He had anemia, to begin with…"

"Do you think I'm stupid? I saw him bleeding out. It soaked through the bandage and dripped onto his pillow and blanket. You mean to tell me that you didn't notice any of that?"

"Look, this is a very busy department. I get ten minutes per deceased on average; this is how much time I have to perform my examination. When I first saw your child, he was already washed. There was no bandage. It must have been removed before. Don't look at me like that. I can't have opinions about my superiors, but I'm honest with you because I'm leaving the country next year… I can only write down what I see, but I saw no external bleeding."

"May I see the tumor that they removed from his ear? I want to look at what killed my son…"

"What do you mean? You want to see the tissue sample? I'll get it for you."

He left and then came back with a blueish smudge on a small piece of glass. Meanwhile, I turned the cassette in the recorder in my pocket.

"Here you go," he said. "This is it."

"Sorry, I didn't ask for this splotch but for the tumor. They said it was a yellowish stretchy thing full of pus. That's what I want to see."

"You must have misunderstood something. The tumor could not be removed because of the severe bleeding. They only took two very small samples."

"Are you telling me that they practically didn't operate on him? That he had to die for this shitty little stain you smeared over a glass? Tell me that's not true. Please."

"Look," he said in a quiet voice, "we also found cancerous cells in other places."

"They had told me that he was 'beyond saving,' but I can't believe that. I'm unable to believe it. He was in perfect physical condition; he was improving, walking, taking stairs, even ran when we held him…"

"The sample taken from the right femur contained 100% cancerous cells."

"And were these cells all alive?"

"No."

"What was the ratio of living and dead cells?"

"About 50-50%."

"So does this mean that the chemotherapy had worked? That he was reacting to it?

"Probably, but we can't know how long he could have endured the treatments."

"Did you find cancer cells anywhere else? Like in his brain, lungs, heart, kidneys or somewhere…?"

"No."

"And what about the bone marrow? They had told us at the end of July that it was in remission, that there were only 2-3% of cancerous cells left. But since the tragedy, the doctors are of the opinion that it never was in remission. How can that be?"

"We used a different method then. I don't know how that could have happened. It's a fact that later, using a different method, they found cancerous nodes in the sample, in about 20-30%."

"So what's the truth? Was he in remission or not?"

"Probably not."

"Can two examinations yield such different results?"

"They are two different methods."

"I feel you're keeping the truth from me. That my son had a chance to recover. Today 95% of children with leukemia can be cured."

"Yes, but your son fell in the remaining 5%. Sorry, but I have to go. I've already spent more time with you than I can afford."

"Wait. I still need to ask you something. Who stole the mobile phone?"

"Excuse me?"

"You probably heard that it disappeared and reappeared later. Did you take it? Are you capable of stealing from a dead baby?"

"It must have been a mistake. They usually don't send things like that here. It's the relatives that have to put personal items into the coffin."

"You all are probably jaded, soulless people who aren't fazed by anything. Did you see the child after the autopsy?"

"The 'restoration' and dressing were done by one of my colleagues."

"So, he was the one who put the phone away. Could I talk to him? I have a few things I'd like to say to that man. You know, I want him to see his child like I did mine. You don't see scenes like this even in a horror movie."

"I'm afraid that's impossible."

"Why?"

"Because a few days after your son's death, he tragically also passed away."

"Oh, my God. It's best that I go now."

I stumbled out of the room and walked along the corridor decorated by innumerable organs floating in formalin. These were all living people once. Maybe Nail's brain is already here floating among them… The morbid thought made me nauseous, so I ran outside to the yard to get some fresh air. I stopped at the first phone booth and angrily, my eyes tearing up, started to dial my lawyer.

"I made my decision: I'm going to sue everyone. You won't believe it; they didn't even do the operation. They only took two small tissue samples. That's why they died. They left the bleeding tumor open because they thought it was a pus node. There is not a word anywhere about the bleeding. They told me that by the time of the autopsy, they hid all evidence. Can you believe it?"

"Come into my office, and bring the autopsy report. We'll write a request to the institution to give out the documentation."

The weeks passed, and my anger grew. Meanwhile, in another interview, I said that I was thinking about suing. My attorney said it was a mistake because it increased the chance that they would give us real documents, final reports, and operation descriptions. Most of these are created post factum.

A forensic expert looked at Nail's autopsy report and said, "The child was either very sick or they really screwed something up."

I'd only change it slightly. He was very sick, AND they screwed up.

I also phoned the blood bank to ask why it took 130 minutes for them to bring over the blood from the building that's less than half a mile from the hospital – the blood that we ordered two days before.

I didn't receive an answer because they ordered a news blackout in connection with our case.

Weeks later, I received the photocopied documents. For some of them, they sent five copies, and they also sent me a $10 bill for photocopying that by law I had to pay.

The documentation was almost complete, with one exception. They forgot to send the report from July, which stated that Nail was in remission. Too bad the professor wrote it on the chart with his own hand.

In every report after that, they stressed that there never was a remission period, so Nail never even had a chance of surviving. But then why the operation?

Questions that I'll never get the answer to.

When I looked at the papers, I started considering our chances. Documentation written post factum, the risky nature of the operation that could always be referred to, papers signed by me stating that they informed me about everything, the blood bank's long, story-like, minute-precise report. A doctor that may really be broken by death and who had a grandson the same age. Doctors who tried to cure Nail but proved to be helpless against the deadly disease. Would it not be easier to accept their explanation rather than fruitlessly fighting the legal teams of hospitals for years?

But does anyone have the right to take the possibility of healing through hope and miracles from someone? Can they destroy faith? Can they force us to live a life filled with self-accusation? Can they put the blame on the parents? Can anyone kill a man's dreams with impunity?

Can a stranger finish the bedtime story I started to read? Can they close the cover of the dream-giving book?

Can they shatter the star of Christmas in our heart when for us, every day is another happy, shining celebration?

These are my rhetorical questions.

I followed the clues, which led me to the directing professor of the children's hospital. The elderly professor behaved very humanely with me and listened to my grievances with empathy, although sometimes with a little short-temper. He tried to answer my professional questions. What's more, he made a phone call to Medical Services to track down a long-awaited test result. He saw that I wasn't lying and honestly told me that although he was the director of the institution, he was not omniscient and couldn't be responsible for the demeanor of his colleagues. He had no spiritual or any other kind of means to force adults to behave differently, to do their job more humanely. Everyone who chooses such a profession has to find that out themselves.

I started crying more than once, the memories hurting me. The professor was suddenly called to the OR. During that time, I spoke to his secretary, who also proved to be understanding.

It didn't mean anything to her, but she told me that after Nail's tragedy, they received a circular from the blood bank obligating them to obtain a fridge specifically for the storage of blood.

"We had one, to begin with, but the hospital where it happened did not, and they also referred to this on account of the tragedy."

I had to smile: what fallible conclusions some people can draw. They secure themselves in advance against a possible legal scandal. So, they didn't have a fridge? Blood is stored at room temperature for hours before use. If not, it has to be heated up.

But at least Nail didn't die in vain – I cried to myself mockingly. The hospitals and patients received a few new fridges.

The professor returned from the OR, and we resumed our talk. He asked me not to make a hasty decision about the possible lawsuit and to speak to the doctor who performed the operation who was devastated by the events.

"Look, believe me, despite what happened, that man is a surgeon with golden hands. I don't believe that there are more skilled otolaryngologists in the country. Hundreds, thousands, owe their life to him, and he would have helped you too if he could. That's the only reason he agreed to the surgery."

"You also agree that our child could not be saved?"

"Look, if somebody told me that this is my only chance to save my child, I would have done it no matter what. Or don't you agree? If there was no other choice…"

"But why didn't they inform us about that? Why were they not honest with us? Professor, believe me, we would never have made this whole scandal if we hadn't been misled. If they had brought the blood – I can't understand why they didn't – if they had been near him and treated him immediately, put him on machines, if they had done everything in their power to save him. But they would have needed the blood. Then I would be a bit calmer and could stand over his grave with a clean conscience knowing that everyone did everything they could. But that wasn't what we had to live through."

"This must be horrible for you as parents. It even shocked us veteran doctors."

"You mean you are bothered by my son's death?"

"How can we not!" he snapped at me. "We all have grandchildren the same age. We are human too."

"That's good to hear. You at least took the time to talk to me like a human being."

"It's nothing. But please find the professor. I'll arrange it for you. You know, there is another sick baby, and only he can help… But he doesn't want to do it because he's been so devastated by this tragedy."

We finally met him in his office the day before All Saints. I went alone. Ruslan thought they had nothing to say to each other. We talked for hours but could not make any progress. The arguments didn't work on either side. It was getting late, and suddenly, there was children's laughter from under the window.

"Papa, Papa…"

"It's my grandson. Please wait a minute." And he hurried to the window to greet them.

First I couldn't swallow. Then I started to cry. Did I have the right to overrule God's judgment? Maybe fate really wanted it this way? And Nail chose his short little life himself? To teach us, to teach the doctors whose path crossed his? I don't know. But what does it matter anymore? I can't have him back anyway.

To let others die because of my son, because they won't even try to help them? Or maybe they draw the consequences and fulfill the dream of other fates, drying up the tears of other parents, families with hope, faith, and healing? I wonder if it really will be like that…

If Nail's death can give a chance to others, then why do I bother with lawsuits and accusations?

I was packing my things, getting ready to go, when the professor unexpectedly turned to me.

"Look, did you see those images I sent you?"

"No, I received no images, only documents, charts, and final records."

"I don't understand. I sent them to our lawyer to post it to you. It seems that for some reasons, they thought this envelope was unimportant. Wait, I'll show you."

He pulled out X-ray images and photos. Then he started cropping them with a pair of scissors.

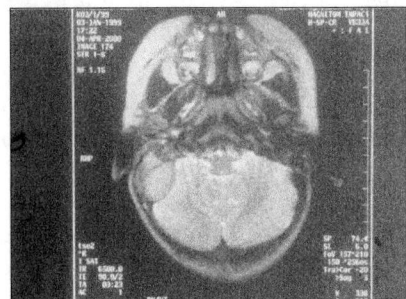

The tumor was small in April

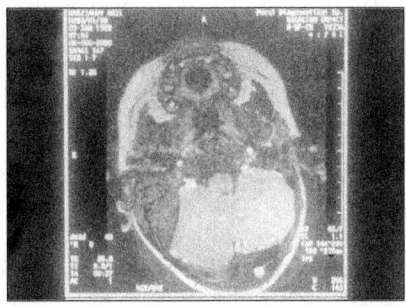

On the X-ray before the operation, the tumor is double the size of the previous stage

"This is an X-ray from April. The dark patch indicates the tumor. It used to be that big. The other image is from September. If I overlap them, you can see the difference. Look closely. What do you see?"

"Well, the tumor has doubled its size, if I'm not mistaken..." I answered.

"Yes, that's right. And it was unstoppable, damaging the bones. It was an extremely malignant tumor."

"But in September, after the MRI scan, we were told that the tumor was in a regressing stage..."

"Ah! That's nonsense. I don't know who said that, but this tumor was growing continuously. I saw it when I compared the two images."

"But you've left it open. You thought it was pus…"

"Yes, the yellowish spongy formation looked like pus." he answered.

"But why couldn't you distinguish between pus and a tumor?"

"This is a common problem with cancerous cells," he explained. "Due to chemotherapy, they often turn into an infected, postulate tissue. This is what I assumed in this case. When I analyzed it under the microscope, I was surprised to see the malignant cells. I've been working in this field for decades, but I've never seen anything like this before. Neither my colleagues…"

"Do you say that Nail would've died anyway? Regardless of the operation?"

"I think so. Within a very short time and in tremendous agony."

"But this is unbelievable," I said miserably. "In my thoughts, I'm still sitting in front of the OR and waiting… I imagine that everything went fine, and we live happily ever after. That he's recovered. That it is just a bad dream, and someone is going to wake me up."

"This is exactly what I feel, too. I've never had a case like that. Most of the time, we're working with adults. I'll never get used to the death of children, even though we have to face tragedies every day. That's why I respect pediatric oncologists."

"How did your colleagues manage to cope with Nail's death?" I asked him.

"It devastated everyone. We spent the first few days in silence. The anesthesiologist, who is a lovely lady, was about to move to the children's clinic. But after what happened, she'll think about it twice, I suppose."

"And what about the young nurse who was crying with us?"

"She's on leave now. She's done," he replied.

"Why don't you employ a professional ICU nurse?"

"We can't afford it. They work as cashiers in plazas because they get more money there. We get the rest. We hire professional nurses from other clinics and pay night shifts," he explained to me. "Just think about it. After an eight, ten, or twelve hour long shift, they come here and provide care for patients with intensive care needs. This is Europe! These are the healthcare conditions in Hungary. There are rumors about closing our facility as well. And I tell you one more thing… One day after you son's death, we had another operation with the exact same team. When we were done with the operation, we transported the man to the ICU. Having learned from the tragedy of the previous day, two or three colleagues stayed with him. He suddenly sat on the bed, coughing and kept asking for some kind of a spray. He didn't inform us about his heart disease. He stopped breathing and was clinically dead. We were shocked. We didn't want to lose another patient. We called the ambulance instantly, and we began CPR. It was successful. He sent him over to the Heart Center for further treatment. In the case of Nail, everything came together. The whole world was against us. I'm deeply sorry."

The next day, I decided not to sue anyone. It would be beneath Nail and me. I was only gathering information out of curiosity. The professor promised me that he'd let me know of any new information about Nail's mysterious disease. As for now, he hasn't written me a single letter. Nail's case is probably long forgotten.

It was raining on All Saints' Day. We slept at my mom's place so that we could visit the cemetery easily. I was inconsolable. I went to Nail's grave several times that day. I decorated his final resting place with white flowers. It felt good to realize that others placed flowers in memory on my son's grave as well.

And the rain was pouring. I always loved rain. I loved its monotonous noise. It washed away the dust from the leaves and pavements. I raised my head, and it washed away my tears and calmed down my raging soul. I missed Nail.

The night fell, and it stopped raining. Crowds were gathering around the graves. Candle lights were dancing everywhere I looked, symbolizing the promise of eternal life. Dark clouds, night and day, the Sun and the Moon, the living and the dead, the scent of flowers and the mouldering bones merged on the horizon. I realized how beautiful passing away is.

Friends came by, and I could see that they were embarrassed. They hardly spoke. Neither of them uttered Nail's name. Otherwise, I was thankful for their visit.

Csingiz wanted to go home. He was tired and cold. I squatted next to Nail's grave and placed all the candles away from the white wooden grave marker. I looked at the myriad of flowers covering the soil, and I slowly stood up. Suddenly, I noticed a dark shadow approaching, holding a bunch of white flowers. She stopped a few meters away and said: "Would you mind?"

I nodded my head, and the nurse came closer. Nail used to call her "Zé" for an unknown reason. She came to the funeral as well and brought the most beautiful wreath I've ever seen. It was made of little white rosebuds, and there was a note written on the ribbon which said: "You'll have laughing stars…" We hadn't seen each other since the funeral. We were engulfed in a hug.

She placed a flower on Nail's grave, lit a candle, and then asked whether I knew that there was a cross or a statue of the Virgin Mary nearby.

"This one is for Nail," she said pointing at the white flower on the grave. "But I couldn't come earlier to visit the others. These are for Krisztián, Gergő, Balázs and Lilla. And the fifth one is for all the other children who died…"

This nurse from the oncology department set an example for her co-workers. She was brave enough to come here. She was brave enough to cry. And she was brave enough to admit that she missed these children.

I watched her leaving, and I promised myself that if I ever had the opportunity, I'd raise a statue as a memento of children who died of cancer or of any other serious illness so that people will have a place where they can bring their flowers and light a candle.

Ruslan had a beautiful dream in November. Nailka visited him and wanted to play with Ruslan. They were throwing paper planes, and Nail brought him his huge but funny plush crocodile he received for his first birthday. Ruslan said that the dream was so real that he almost fell off the bed as he was trying to catch the paper plane.

The festive season was a turbulent time for us. I wasn't prepared for such grief. Every Christmas decoration, handmade ornament, and Santa Claus made me cry. I don't know how I survived the holidays.

I found my safe place in reading. I was still interested in death, especially the different stages of death.

Csingiz had changed a lot. He was happy, lively and always smiling. In November, I told him that I was pregnant. According to the ultrasound, my baby was just four weeks old, but I knew that this new life was a gift from God.

I kept my pregnancy secret. Csingiz was the first one I told about the baby. He was delighted. He even talked a little about Nail as well.

"Mom, I knew that he'll come back," he said, and his eyes were full of hope. "An angel told me. And then you will be happy forever, and you won't be visiting the cemetery all the time, right?"

"We should always respect Nail," I replied pointing at his photo. "When he returns to us, we'll be able to identify him only by his soul, but he'll be living in a different body. It might be a body of a girl or a boy. I'll be much more happier, but I'll never forget Nail."

"Okay, this is fantastic. I can't wait!"

"What do you think? Is it a boy or a girl?"

"I don't know," he replied. What do you think?

"I have a pendulum. Let's ask it."

I held the string, and we started to ask yes and no questions.

"Are we getting Nail back?"

"Yes."

"Is it a boy?"

"Yes."

"Is it a girl?"

"No."

"Does he look like Nail?"

"Yes."

Csingiz liked this game. I handed him the pendulum, but it didn't move in his hand.

"Don't take it too seriously," I whispered inconsolably. "This is just a game, my darling. The pendulum might be wrong."

"I don't think so," he replied. "Why would the pendulum lie to us?"

"I don't know. We'll see."

I told the big news to Ruslan and then to my mom. It was our secret. I burst into tears every time I had to visit the gynecologist.

On December 20, Nail appeared in my dreams. He was sitting in my lap, and he resembled his old self. There was his great-grandmother and one of his aunts with us.

We spent Christmas together at my mother's. We also slept there. It would've been unbearable for us to stay at home. I didn't want to decorate the tree, but I had to do it for Csingiz. We put the ornaments up on the tree together. Only angels; no stars, no candles, no sparklers and no tree topper.

I could only think about Nail and last year's Christmas. His only Christmas. When I got home – we'd been working that day – I lifted him up and put him on my lap. We were opening the presents together, but his eyes were fixed on the sparkling festive lights. He kept moving his little body for a deeply rooted rhythm of life, smiling. We even have it on videotape.

But this year, it was Christmas time without Nail. I was thinking about placing his photo under the tree, but I changed my mind. We were not ready for that. Although I made a little present for him and signed every Christmas card in his name as well.

We went to the cemetery and put a tiny decorated tree on Nail's grave. We went back to my mother's place, and I left Csingiz with her.

I returned to the grave later at night. I wanted to see the lights.

I wiped my tears away before entering the house. I didn't have right to spoil others' holiday.

I couldn't sleep that night. I was standing by the window for long hours and watched the sky, the stars, and the light of the street lamps.

I got up early before sunrise. I packed a few candles and went out to the cemetery. It was just me walking on the frozen pavement. My body was trembling. I began to run. When I reached the grave, I threw myself onto the heap of flowers covering my son's dead body.

I'd been crying and shouting for one and a half hours. I was raging madly. I didn't have to behave myself, and I let my rage out. I let my pain out. I let the endless flood of my tears out. I was beating the frozen ground with my bare fists until it hurt. I wanted it to hurt. I was biting my mouth until I could feel the metallic taste of blood in my mouth. I hated the whole world. I hated myself. I hated Nail for leaving me.

I couldn't stop crying. The absence of my son had become physically unbearable. I'd reached the lowest point from where there was no return.

I never thought that there would be times when I was lying on my son's grave, talking madly to his grave marker. I hugged the cold wooden cross, and I returned among the living…

On December 30, I woke up terrified from a disturbing nightmare. I had to change clothes since my nightgown was soaking wet.

Nail would've been two years old on January 3. I thought I should bring him a little cake with two candles for his birthday, but I changed my mind because I knew it would disappear. Thieves were stealing everything from the cemetery: flowers, ornaments, crosses, vases. When our beautiful wreath was stolen, I kept looking for it among the parcels.

People are weird. They are dehumanized. They don't feel bad about stealing from an infant's grave anymore.

Many stole out of business interest. They came organized, with bikes and bags, making their rounds and stopping here and there. They delivered upon request and most of the time knew what to look for and where. Many florists pay good money for the flowers and accessories they used to make their wreaths. But they take other things, too: anything they can possibly sell. Little candles, larger candles, crosses, doves, vases, marble slates…

Many shopkeepers take them back.

I tried to make a complaint at the Funeral Services. They said there was nothing they could do. They couldn't station a security guard next to every corpse. Yes, I agree with that, but they could take other measures. For example, they could check the people who leave the cemetery with fully stuffed bags.

"Why do you bother?" said another broken, grieving parent, who'd been coming here visiting his dead child for years.

I admitted it was a pointless fight against a group of petty thieves. Instead, I followed the advice of veteran grievers. I had all flowers cut short, had Nail's name written into each of the silk flowers and put them in a less prominent place. I was quite happy with the frost because it meant that the flowers I brought would freeze until the next day and prove less alluring to the thieves. They dug up any shrubs, evergreens, pansies, rooted and bulbous flowers I planted, and I'd had just about enough of this. I asked Funeral Services for permission to build a fence around the grave, but they denied it saying that it was against the law. But what kind of law allows for the infringement of the funerary rights of both the living and the dead?

This was the main reason why I didn't bring a real cake for him that day. The wreath with tiny grapes, butterflies, ladybugs and a ribbon saying, "We will love you forever…" would have to do.

I would never wish on anyone to "celebrate" their child's birthday in a cemetery. It is a cruel feeling. After we had stopped crying, I thought about what Nail would look like today. Does time pass at all over there? Does his ghost remain twenty months old forever, or will it keep growing forever as time passes? If anyone knows, please write it to me…

I think he'll stay the same forever: a twenty month-old missed chance for the fulfillment of an adult life.

After my Christmas outburst, I was feeling somewhat better.

Following peaceful periods, I usually sank back into my depression. I tried to look strong on the outside, but this calmness was like a house of cards. It kept falling apart at the most banal things. If I saw a child of similar age, or a mother who beat or handled her child roughly, I was instantly back on the ground. But everyday happenings such as a bus driver waiting for a mother and child, or if anyone spoke a kind and humane word to me, drove me to crying. I usually bought my flowers opposite the cemetery's main entrance at the same florist at a discount price because they knew I was bringing them for Nail. I wasn't buying them there to save money but because the gesture warmed my heart every time.

During the second week of January, I got a letter.

Recently, I turned to a shaman fortune teller from Százhalombatta for help. I've read several books written by this woman, and I knew that she was in connection with the spiritual world. I didn't need the complete computer analysis; I just wanted to get answers to my questions from Nailka.

I wasn't expecting such a quick answer.

Here's a short extract from the medium's handwritten letter:

> "Dear Madam,
>
> I've received your letter. I'm deeply saddened by the loss that you and your family have encountered. Everything was written in his Karma. He chose you for his embodiment. His short stay on this Earth and his quick leaving had two main objectives:
>
> The first one was to fulfill his life plan – even if it was a very short one.
>
> Secondly, via his tragedy, he wanted to call your attention to the meaning of our existence. He wanted to set an example by his early death.
>
> I know that it might be upsetting to read my letter, but I have to be honest with you.
>
> You child has extraordinary spiritual capacities. Before his birth, he was destined to make sacrifices for your development. His self-sacrifice was part of the plan. On the photo of him in the pram, I can see great wisdom and anxiety in his eyes. He knew exactly what had been written in his Karma.
>
> He DIDN'T feel pain or fear when he left this Earth. His spiritual friends have been waiting for him. He's not in the lightness. He's in an intermediate world, waiting for something. He's not mad at you for trying to keep him staying with you during the CPR.
>
> It has been written in the plan that he had to die. This is why that medical team has been chosen for his operation. It wasn't medical malpractice – it was all planned. Don't blame them, and don't blame yourself. It would only make your son's self-sacrifice meaningless.
>
> You son is with the Virgin Mary now! She's taking care of him.
>
> He hasn't met Jesus because it was written the plan. He's not angry with you at all! (I'm answering your question in the original order.)
>
> You son has a plan: he's about to return to your life but he needs to recover from this trauma, and your family needs to change and develop spiritually.

Now I see no chance to get rid of your debt. Your child didn't want to recover (on the spiritual level) since it wasn't part of his life plan. Therefore, you should've avoided putting yourselves into this financial burden, but I know that parents would do anything for their child.

Your spiritual reserves are depleting; you need to collect your strength.

Nail has a message for all of you: he wants you to let him go and don't cry for him. Otherwise, you would be pulling him back on this Earth and risking him transforming into a ghost. It would take a lot of energy for him to fight against your adherence.

You need to let him go.

The identical dates of his birth and death (13:50 p.m.) also had a meaning: it has happened as planned.

The pathologist died of natural causes. His death can't be explained otherwise.

Two of your family members will follow Nail. I'm talking about spiritual family, not physical. (Spiritual family members are not necessarily blood relatives.) We don't know who these two persons will be. You, Nail, and your son are members of the same spiritual family, but your husband is not part of this spiritual group.

Dear Madam, I won't accept any money for this analysis because it would contradict my principles. I know what you feel. I've lost my parents and three brothers. I suggest that you listen to your son's message and let him go. You're not in the same physical dimension anymore. You have to understand this.

He didn't want to stay any longer. It wasn't part of his spiritual plan.

If you love him, you let him go. This is what he asks for you as a family – and for you as his mother, particularly. Concentrate on life because you have things to do in this world and not in the realm of the dead.

Yours sincerely, ...XY..."

I read the letter once, and then I read it again and again...

It touched my heart. It is true? Is my son with the Virgin Mary now? She didn't betray Nail. My prayers had been heard.

There were times when I suspected that my son might be guarded by the Virgin Mary, but it seemed absurd. Could I trust the words of the medium?

Is Nail in a safe place? This is what I want. The Virgin Mary is the one who can protect and teach him.

Reading the letter made calm. It made me believe in myself and my feelings. My inner restlessness disappeared, and I was 100% sure that Nail was still with us.

I thought back to the funeral and realized that everything happened for a reason: he gave strength to my crushed soul at the ceremony, and his hideous face in death was a sign for me that the living soul has left his body behind. He shed his earthly body, and he wanted to let me know that he wasn't there.

And there was the piece of music I found and the blue car on the photo… Too many coincidences.

One day after the funeral, my mom told me a strange story that she heard from our neighbor. She was home on the day of the funeral. When we left the house, a little bird landed on the balcony railing and hadn't moved until we got back from the cemetery. Then it flew away.

I was thankful to the shaman fortune teller for her encouraging words and noble gesture. It was very helpful.

That night, before I went to bed, I thought about Nail.

"Could it be possible that the Virgin Mary is taking care of my son?" I asked myself. "Forgive my doubts, my Lord."

I had a dream that night, giving an answer to my question. I've even written a note in my diary to keep the memory of January 13 alive.

I was visited by the Virgin Mary in my dream that night. I followed her, running up a spiral staircase in a tower, leading me to another world. I knew it was her. I didn't dare to look at her bare feet. I was embarrassed, but she smiled at me. I followed her to the top (it was some kind of a bar), and she offered me a seat. I sat down, still breathing heavily after climbing the stairs.

She introduced me to Jesus, who was also sitting at our table. He gave me a mysterious smile but didn't say anything. His hair was shorter than I expected.

I asked them when I could meet Nail.

Mary looked at me as if she had been waiting for this question and said: "Soon. When he's ready…"

It seemed that I was peeping through a keyhole to another world. I knew that all of my questions could've been answered. But I chose to ask only about Nail.

I woke up and sat up in my bed. I couldn't distinguish between dream and reality. It was just a few minutes, but I was really there in the tower. I knew it was real.

I took a pen and paper and quickly wrote down everything so that I could remember my dream later. I fell asleep again.

I was holding Nailka in my hands, and I felt immense happiness.

"I knew I hadn't lost you," I told him.

I looked up at the sky and said, my lips trembling: "Thank you, thank you, thank you…"

When I woke up in the morning, I was still enchanted by the dream. I couldn't erase my smile.

It was interesting that Csingiz and Ruslan also had a dream with Nail that night. Ruslan's dream was about Nail's death and rebirth. The "new Nail" resembled his old self. Csingiz didn't go into details – he never did – just said that Nail visited him the night before, he loves everybody, and "he will be a boy" (referring to my unborn child).

From that moment on, I believed that the Virgin Mary was taking care of my child.

However, despite the comfort in that one particular dream, I had other dreams about Nail that were disturbing. I also had a call from my aunt. She said that she read the cards (my aunt was a fortune teller) and told me: I'm going to die soon." "I have nine to eighteen months left."

I was falling into a depression again. I hated the nights. I was afraid to fall asleep, and I was afraid of my dreams as well. I used meditation to overcome the hardships. I started re-reading my books about death. I realized that I had only one choice: making an alliance with death.

I sat down and said: "Okay, death. You won, I admit. You outnumbered us, but I'm not mad at you. I know that you're not that hideous, and you're guarding my son somewhere. I wanted to enter your realm, but this is not the time. Please be my guide and show me the way to my son in the afterlife."

I sat on the bed with my back to the cold wall. I looked into the eyes of Nail's portrait on the opposite wall and started talking to him.

"My dear son, I love you very much. Forever, like I promised. Nothing can ever separate us. I will not bother you anymore or put my pain on you. I won't send cries, but my heart that beats for you. My unconditional, true and faithful love will find you wherever you are. And by it, you'll know that I'm always waiting for you, and you can come to me anytime you want to. So, I let you on your way and leave it to you to decide whether you want to come back. No one's forcing you especially not me, your mother. Thank you that you chose me. You brought me the happiest days of my life. Now the decision rests with you, but I want you to know that I'll keep a room for you in my heart where you can return any time and for as long as you want, or you can hide there if you're hurt, or you just feel like it. I love you; I love you. I love you forever through eternity…"

I sent out a mental energy ray toward him. A few moments later, I felt my brow pleasantly tingle. I didn't see it but knew instantly that Nail's hand was stroking me.

I switched off my mind and let the feeling wash over me. Tears soaked my face, but nothing mattered.

How long had I been waiting for this moment? Was it eternity or only six months? Maybe it never left me, or was my grief simply too much for me to notice?

And what did it take?

Nothing but to accept and tame the dreadful death. To not look at it as an enemy but as a companion; to let my actions be governed by my love instead of my hate. My mind enlightened: Nail was here with me from the first moment and never left me. Because death can't break up true love. Maybe it doesn't even want to. What is death? The beginning of a new life in an incorporeal unknown dimension? Is it not a closed trap door, but a gate guarding the altar of eternity? Not dark blackness but a snow white sunrise on the horizon? The Eden of mysteries? A world where the cost of admittance is the sacrifice of our old beliefs and hearts pounding with sad physical feelings?

I can't know. But it is a fact: The heavens brought Nail back to me. The only thing that hurt is that no matter how softly I hugged and kissed, I could no longer feel the irreplaceable wonder of physical touch. Our connection was on a whole new level now.

From this time, he came regularly and showed me he'd not left me. At first, I burst out crying whenever he appeared because he could pop in at the most unexpected moments out of nothing, and I really missed his little body…

There was no system to the time we spent together. Sometimes he was with me for hours multiple times a day; other times he didn't show for days. The tingling on my forehead and at the base of my hair became more accentuated every time. I started sensing when a soul visited me, but none of them came with ill intentions. I felt protected; the evil spirits didn't bother me. The top of my head, forehead, and nape still pulsated and vibrated but not the same way, so I knew it wasn't my son. I never sent any of them away and thanked them for helping me from the afterlife. I couldn't really communicate with them; my role was restricted to sensing them. Maybe when I'm more along the road toward them, I can begin to understand them. But I won't force it because that world also has its own rules… I just let them lead me if I'm lost or come to a complicated crossroads.

Immediately after I could contact Nail, things around me changed. The most pleasant surprise came in my dreams. The nightmares slowly lost their strength, and as soon as they realized that I wasn't desperate anymore, they disappeared from my life more than a year ago now.

My attention slowly shifted from death to life; I wanted more and more to meet with the one I carried in my womb.

Spring came, and I watched nature's rebirth with open eyes. I was mesmerized by the process. I saw beauties I never saw before and soaked it up like a dry sponge does water. I can't say that I was never sad or never cried after that, but the intense pain in me turned into a delighted, graceful sadness.

I was becoming calmer. Nail's physical absence lessened but didn't go away completely. I could no longer completely recall his unique baby smell like I could before.

My grief transformed. I remember the first fit of madness when the tragedy happened, and I thought I died with him. I vegetated as a living dead as long as the fog-like shell from the shock remained. Then after a few moments, it burst and in came raging revenge, pointless fighting, and self-torturing accusations. I woke up, and with the help of the power of God, I took our fate back into my hands. If I got stuck, I didn't get desperate because I knew that Nail's light would light my path, and I only needed to follow my heart where he imprinted himself.

I contacted the companies we were heavily indebted to and tried to ask for time to come up with the money. I probably don't need to say where they told me to go… Because according to them, we already had plenty of time.

The bank arrears at that time exceeded millions of dollars, and so did our debts. Our shop was almost empty, and I didn't know what to do. I prayed for help.

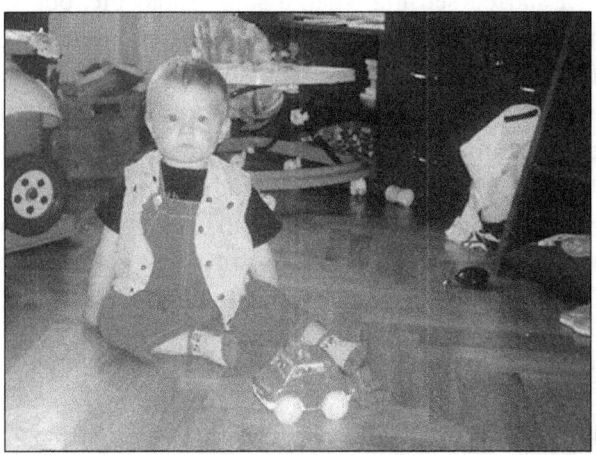

Rinát means "reborn" in Tatar

Within a few days, two of our employees quit, one of whom was my brother. I wasn't really surprised that he too had betrayed me. We'd lost lots of our friends, suppliers, and clients. Most of them disappeared from our life right after Nail's death. People – especially those with young children – avoided us like the plague. They were afraid of us. Of course, their reaction increased my remorse and isolation, though I admit that I wasn't the best talking partner with my tear-stained face.

I let them go. I didn't want to beg for anyone's friendship. As time passed, new friends arrived who didn't care about our poverty and vulnerability.

Several family members cut ties with us. My mother and my grandmother were the only ones who supported us even by taking loans.

I had to spend the third trimester of pregnancy in hospital. I needed to take insulin injections four times a day due to my diabetes, and I also had problems with my liver. The majority of the doctors, nurses, and patients behaved humanely.

My doctors were monitoring my baby's development with frequent ultrasound scans. I began to realize that I was going to be a mother again. Sometimes, I was feeling depressed. I was walking a lot in the nearby park, which was very close to the clinic where the fate of my little son had been sealed. I could see the ICU from my window. And I could see the garden where we used to pick flowers. On my worst days, I turned to the wall in my bed, leafing through old photo albums. I was consumed by waiting. I got tired of medical examinations. I wanted to go home to Csingiz, who was terrified by the thought that I would leave him.

But at least I was safe here. I escaped from harassing, demanding and blackmailing letters and calls. I could deliver my baby in relative peace.

I was thirty-seven weeks pregnant on June 28, 2001. I was considered to be at full term, and I was going to give birth to a huge baby. My liver started to give up. I was itchy, I had nausea, and my internal organs were almost blowing up. I asked for permission to initiate the birth. We had to wait for the thirty-seventh week for my baby not to be considered premature.

That morning I went into the OR alone... almost alone. Nail was there with me. I had photos of him under my pillow.

My husband was somewhere between Hungary and Russia. He had to fly home to earn some money. My mom was waiting outside. Csingiz and my father were at home, waiting for the big news.

It was my hardest labor ever. At 3 o'clock p.m., Rinát Noel arrived.

I named him Rinát because it means "reborn." And I named him Noel because it means "gift bringer" and also sounds similar to Nail.

Csingiz was the first I called.

"Happy birthday, darling. You got the most precious present in the world. When you grow up, I hope you'll understand. Your little brother was born," I said, emotions swirling inside me. I could hardly speak.

My mom stepped into the room, and I had to turn my head away. I didn't want her to see my tears. I felt the most profound, overwhelming joy and, at the same time, an all-consuming sadness.

I put down my baby on the bed at home. Ruslan and Csingiz crouched down beside the newcomer. After a few minutes, my husband opened his mouth, saying: "I can't believe we are four of us again!"

At the time, Rinát's broad smile and the shining light of his blue eyes made me believe in the miracle of reincarnation.

Epilogue

Nail's death changed my life forever. Now I see that it wasn't in vain. I can decode his messages and live my life accordingly, following my instincts. I've got to learn to appreciate the little things in life like a nice gesture, an encouraging word, a flower, a hug. Nail pushed the deceitful parasites and opportunists away from us.

In return, fantastic friends, helpful officers, selfless consultants and empathetic fellow sufferers landed in my life.

I've learned how to put my pride aside and how to say goodbye to things that don't matter anymore.

I sold my long-collected home library and most of my clothes. My children have always had everything they needed.

I'm thankful for the toys, children's clothes and furniture that we received from our friends. I value the importance of people we can count on.

I had to understand that large organizations won't open doors to ordinary citizens. I've sent letters to more than fifty organizations worldwide – only two of them replied.

Probably, our prime minister hasn't received my letter and the excerpt from this manuscript. That's okay. I've realized that a good lawyer can help me get back on my feet and financial institutions are open for discussions if I'm persistent enough, even though I'm not a millionaire.

And, last but not least, my childhood dream has come true thanks to Nail: I've started to write my book.

I've realized that I have a mission to complete in the non-profit sector.

By fate and on behalf of Nail's memory, I want to help people. This is why I established the Light of Eyes Foundation that offers help for children with palliative care needs and for their families as well.

Our mission is to take part in the creation of the legislative background of children's hospice and to open the first children's hospice house (Dóri Ház) in Hungary.

We are also planning to organize a transport service for sick children because currently these children with weak immune systems are being transported by crowded ambulances, together with adult patients.

I consider it important to create a memorial site in the cemetery that family members can visit – regardless of when their child died or what their connection with the deceased is. There are a lot of families in Hungary who had stillborn babies. According to the current legislation, these parents can't bury their child or ever see the baby. This is why it is so important to create a place where families can honor and remember children who have died.

My dream is to build a brand new, purpose-built children's hospice facility (Butterfly Children's Hospice House) in the town of Romonya near Pécs. The construction is expected to be finished by December 31, 2020 – depending on sufficient funding. The children's hospice complex itself will cost an approximate net amount of $5 million US dollars. I'm ready to build Hungary's first, professional children's hospice of a model value for the quasi 16,000 touched families.

Pécs, February 20, 2001

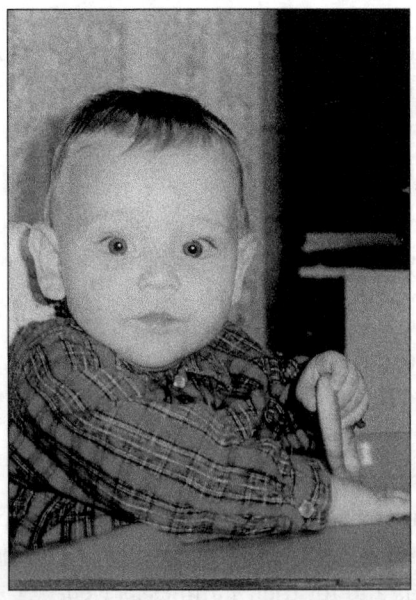

Nailka's t-shirt is an eternal memento
Rinát (1) and Csingiz (8) were born on the same day

Afterword

SEVENTEEN YEARS AFTER NAIL'S DEATH

The Light of My Eyes Foundation has accomplished its mission: ambulance cars, children's hospice house, and the Angels' Passage.

After Nail's death, my grief became pathological. What does it mean? I was unable to cope with my pain and loss. I couldn't "fill up" empty space he left behind. It took me seven years to recover from the death of Nail and to be able to function as a mother and a woman again. It took me that long to be able to bake cookies for my children.

I think the hardest part was the remorse. I'm still not over it. I will never be. In some respects, I felt I was responsible for what happened to Nail. I still think about the "What would have happened if?" questions, and my subconscious mind is still searching for the answers. I couldn't let it go. It took me about ten years to stop asking myself, "Why?", "Why me?", "Why us?", "Why Nail?" I passed the unanswered questions to the universe and accepted that I might only get my answers beyond when we would be together again. At our reunion.

When, after so many years, I happen to talk about Nail's death, I still feel the guilt, my part in losing him. Because people defend themselves with this after all these days. This is their shield, their invisible armor that protects them from ever having to face such a pain again. Because it's easier this way…

I slowly realized all my plans:

In 2003 I created the Eternal Child monument in the Pécs Cemetery's children's parcel. Then in 2010, I created the Angels' Passage in the same place, which was Hungary's first ornamental fountain dedicated to the dissemination of children's ashes under one year of age. It's, of course, free for the parents although we have to pay the cemetery a fee after every ceremony. Well, that's how it is.

In 2004 I instituted a child-patient-transport, which is also unique in Hungary, and it only exists in our county. It would be nice to extend it to the whole country, but I don't have enough ambulances and money to plan and maintain it. Now there are 60,000 children we have to potentially transport 24/7, whom the state sponsors by supplying around $2,000 a year. The rest has to be provided by the foundation. Our ambulances run many miles each year, so we're always happy to receive another one.

And believe it or not, in 2010 I opened Hungary's first, little, 70 square mile Hospice House for children in Pécs: the Dóri House. So far we helped more than 150 families. The institute is too small and not equipped to care for incurable children as there isn't even an elevator, and we can only care for two children at a time.

Hungary's second child-hospice house, the Tabhita House in Budapest, was also created and operated by me until Rinát got sick in 2012. Then the owner of the property – our former sponsor – unilaterally pushed me out of the project and has been operating it since. Of course, there is great need for the house there too, and although they deny this, I am happy having created the Tabhita.

There are almost 16,000 families in Hungary in need of care for sick children. This year I started a completely new project: I bought a 25 square mile property outside of town where I'm planning to build a real child-hospice house with two nursing departments, eight and six beds each. One for children, one for young adults. The complex will have a therapy wing with hydrotherapy pool, physiotherapy room, multisensory room, etc., a place for grieving, a funerary room and an ecumenical prayer room. We plan on building two separate apartments for families, and huge open common areas where we can have celebrations.

The symbol for children's hospice is a butterfly; it symbolizes the ethereal, light, death, transformation and metamorphosis.

Rinát's cavalry– our life repeats itself…
We're fighting for a second time: our smallest child got diagnosed with cancer twelve years later to the day.

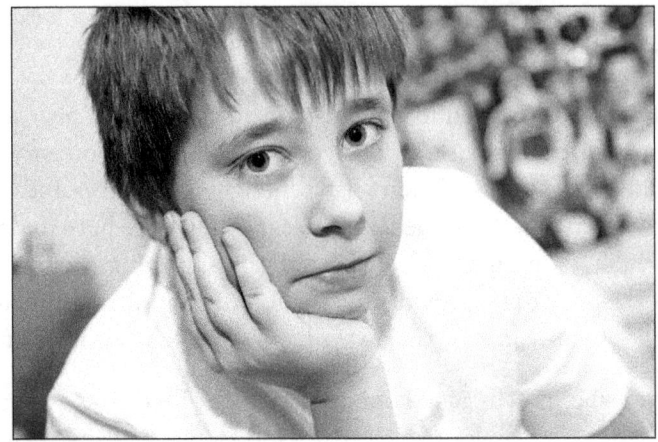

Back then Rinát didn't look like he was fighting a deadly disease

It was the 20th of March 2012. I'll never forget that day as long as I live.

The night before I had a moment of intuition. We were driving back from Törökbálint to Pécs after one of our usual three weekly trips, and I had been very exhausted. I'd already opened the second children's hospice, and the 200 km long commute took a lot of energy out of me. And things were not turning out like I wanted them to. We almost made it back home when on the outskirts of Pécs, we stopped to buy gas. It was late night, and my husband was angrily talking to me on the phone. He told me that our ten-year-old son, Rinát, was having strong pains in his legs.

A bit of history: it was around Christmas when I first noticed that Rinát's legs were hurting. During that time, he'd just started going to basketball training where he first felt the pain during running.

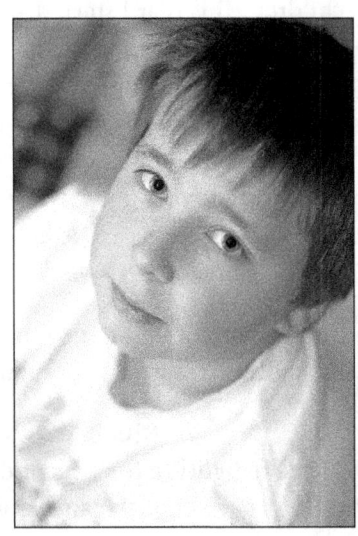

> *I would have killed for him if I had to. Our pain had reached intolerable levels. My husband, my other son, and I fanatically believed in Rinát and fought for his healing as one. When I had no other choices left, I gave up my pride and announced to the world that we were in trouble and needed help.*

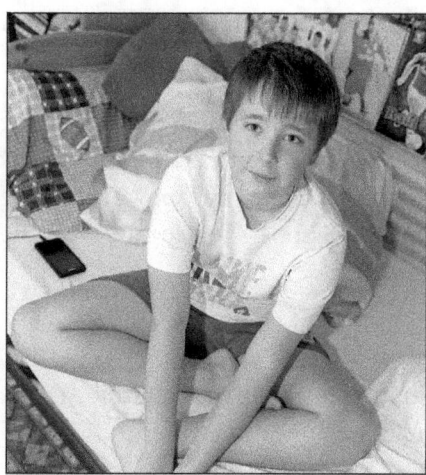

Rinát's will to live gave me strength too. Here he'd already known that his treatment in Mexico was ineffective, but he was still smiling. I've never seen anybody fight as fiercely as him.

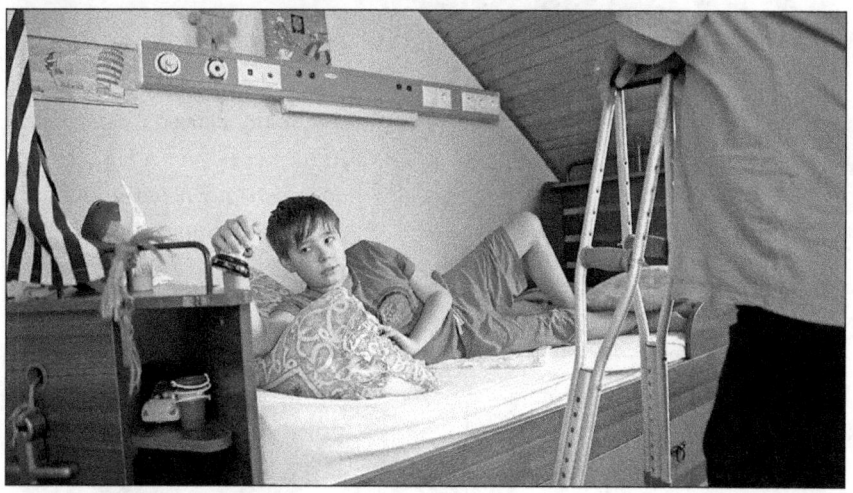

At the beginning of his sickness, he could walk with crutches despite his pain.

At the beginning, his coach thought that he didn't really want to run and that's why he said he was tired. He wanted to refute this, so he kept going to training despite the pain until one day, on the parent-child match held during Christmas, he was limping so hard he couldn't even get on the course.

During Christmas, we spent a weekend on Balatonfüred where he again told us his leg was hurting.

On the first workday of January, we took him to the children's hospital in Pécs where they performed an ultrasound of his legs but couldn't see anything out of the ordinary. They only told us to temporarily stop the training and the PE lessons.

And now, two months later, I received a phone call where my husband in a panicked voice tells me that Rinát has serious pain...

A few weeks before, the condition had improved. He wasn't even complaining much. But because sports played such an important part in his life, my husband and I didn't want our son to stay at home unhappy because he couldn't go on basketball training and PE lessons. He had just tried the basketball hoop when my husband called.

It all hit me in a moment.

I don't know from where, from how deep, from whom the realization came, but in that instant, I knew that my child had bone cancer.

One of the side effects of chemotherapy is the so-called moon face caused by steroids. Rinát never gave up; he optimistically believed in his healing all along.

Rinát with one of his favorite football players: Torres from Chelsea, 2013

I called our child oncologist friend from the petrol station and told him what I was thinking. He tried to calm me, tell me that I was only seeing things because of the trauma we lived through with Nail. Nevertheless, he suggested that we go to the hospital the next morning, on 20 March, for an X-ray. His colleagues would call him immediately in case of any oncological suspicion, he added...

The next day, Rinát had an X-ray.

He was about to leave the room when the assistant shouted after him to go back because they had to do some more scans.

At that moment, I felt crushed inside. I felt and I knew that my child was sick. When the door opened, I heard a voice telling us to go to the oncology department right away…

I didn't ask anything. My body was going into a state of shock. I called my husband and told him that we'd be waiting for him at the oncology. When he arrived, he saw us sitting on a bench in front of the building where Nail had been treated twelve years ago with leukemia. We never wanted to see this place again. And here we were… He got out of the car and started shouting at me. "Barbara, what the hell are we doing here?"

I couldn't put together a meaningful answer. I only told him that Rinát had a tumor…

At that moment, I realized that it was 20 March.

Twelve years earlier on this day, Nailka was diagnosed with cancer. And now our life repeated itself. The doctors found bone cancer in Rinát's body. They ordered diagnostic imaging tests.

We spent the next few days in screaming pain.

We had a supporter at the foundation whom we could count on, a millionaire businessman. I knew that Laci would help us. He was my only hope. God sent him to us for a reason…

When I told Laci about Rinát's condition, he reacted just like everybody else. He said that I was overreacting, and Rinát was going to be fine, nothing serious. He didn't believe me. But months later, my suspicion was verified by the tissue sample tests…

Interestingly, when I needed Laci the most, something had changed in our relationship. We moved away from each other. It happened gradually just like during our first tragedy with Nail: we were left alone. People avoided our family like the plague.

I met one of my old classmates one day. When she noticed me, she crossed to the other side of the road and passed me by. I knew that she was embarrassed. Her reaction was a typical self-defense against the contagious calamity that our family represented. We were cursed; we were called a damned family. They made up theories about the reasons behind our tragedies. They made it easier for themselves to cope with this situation. They placed themselves above us on an ethical level so that they could certify their immunity against similar tragedies.

If it is written in your fate, it will find you. You don't have to be a serial killer or the most evil man in the world to be doomed.

Our wealthy supporter was a deeply religious person. Or at least he considered himself to be a truly religious man. He knows the Bible by heart, and he attends the Sunday mass every week. We had different concepts of a lot of things, but I believe that we respected each other's opinion. I don't consider myself a lesser believer just because I don't go to church every week or I can't quote complete passages from the Bible. We simply had different concepts of faith. Mine was a deeper, more profound and pure faith. I believed in a higher power, in an underlying system of truth, in God, in the universe, in fatality.

My faith is similar to that of Neale Donald Walsch. In his Conversations with God, he writes that he doesn't need an interpreter to understand God's message. We have to find the path that leads us to God within ourselves. This revelatory moment might be a happy experience, a hopeful event, or a ruthless tragedy.

In this matter, by the way, I never agreed with Laci…

He considered himself a more faithful believer because he'd been living with wealth and blessing. He was sure that God was going to let him into his heaven but not me. According to his opinion, I was not good enough for that grace.

I knew that last year's pain and tragedy had negative effects on our relationship. He used to believe in us…

Moreover, he was our greatest supporter. The supporter of my foundation and of my son. I can't thank him enough. But on the day when I told him about Rinát's disease, something had changed forever.

Maybe because of his fears. Or of his belief system, misdoubting my abilities and strength. He started to build a wall between us, brick by brick.

The first sign of the break in our relationship was his decision to look for someone else for the chairman's position at the Tabitha Hospice right after I'd told him about Rinát. He and his wife sat down with one of our social workers at the Tabitha and offered her the position. I was speechless. They stabbed me in the back. They were trying to find a solution for our problems without asking me or without taking my situation into consideration.

Rinát and I. Mother and son, in the Fall of 2011.

Roles and boundaries began to blur, and I ceased to function as the chairman of the foundation. My vulnerability and financial dependence paralyzed me, and I was unable to stand up for myself. My supporter paid the employees' wages, and I had less and less authority over everyday operations. Our negotiations failed to realize, and I had to make compromises. But this was the only way I could ensure the future of the foundation, the hospice house, and Rinát's treatment. There was nothing to do but to take it, to endure the humiliation.

The total cost of our trip to Mexico – I took Rinát to Tijuana for a six-week long Gerson immunotherapy – was covered by my supporter and his wife. I couldn't be more thankful.

When we left, I put them in charge of managing the foundation since I didn't have enough time and energy for that job.

We returned full of hope after the treatment. I believed that the Gerson immunotherapy would be enough for his recovery. I hoped that amputation, operation, and chemotherapy wouldn't be necessary.

My hopes lasted for three weeks – during this time, I was trying to normalize the connection between my sponsor and me. I failed. He had completely different views and kept searching for someone else for my position in the foundation. He wanted someone whom he could control and who acted according to his wish.

He called a meeting at the office and issued an ultimatum. I was under enormous pressure and couldn't stop crying. It wasn't fair. It was below the belt. His behavior was not worthy of a Christian at all. He was blackmailing me. There was a woman – the wife of an ex-government spokesman – whom he wanted to be my successor. She gave a presentation about the foundation and the untapped financial possibilities. She believed that she would be much more suitable for the leader position at the Light of My Eyes Foundation than me. Her presentation in itself was ridiculous. She promised more significant media coverage, but everything she said was based on absurd data. My sponsor was in role confusion. It was my foundation. It was me who established it in remembrance of my son... Therefore, this foundation was my child. It belonged to me.

I told him what I thought, but I couldn't convince him. At the same time, I knew that I needed him. I needed his financial support. Therefore, I had no choice but to humiliate myself in front of my colleagues. He called me useless and wayward. He said that I'd played away my last opportunity. I felt terrible.

A few weeks later, things got even worse.

Rinát's pain intensified. We took him to the children's clinic. The X-ray scan showed that the tumor had grown and reached his knee.

We were shocked, and we kept screaming and shouting with each other for days. We envisioned our whole family getting into a car and crashing into a lorry in a head-on collision. It was simply too much. We were close to giving up. We spent the following weeks in a zombie-like state. Everything was dark and distant. We were confused. I don't know how we could get up every morning. I felt pain and horror in every little cell of my body. We didn't know how much time we had left.

I was sitting on an emotional rollercoaster. Conflicting feelings of despair and the sense of the fact that Rinát needs me were swirling inside me. His struggle to fight kept me alive. I knew that I had to do this. Anything. I was ready to do whatever it took.

In my recent desperate moments, I'd been browsing the Internet at night, trying to find treatment for my son. To look up places where he could have at least 1% more chance of survival. In Hungary, my objections were not toward the doctors and their methods – I knew that they would do everything at their disposal to save Rinát. But I had a deadly experience when back in 2000 my other son died in my arms in a patient room labeled ICU without any supervision. I couldn't ignore this fact, nor did I want to.

My problems were with the circumstances, so I decided to take Rinát to a place where there was more professional experience available because they treated more similarly diagnosed patients.

This made the Hungarian children-oncologists go mad. If they ever read this book, I'll gladly tell them that this had nothing to do with them or me. I absolutely respect their superhuman effort and the overtime they put in to save Hungarian children with cancer. I also know that great people achieved some awesome results despite the bad circumstances. And this whole thing – that made me a persona *non grata* among the children-hospice movement represented by me and children-oncologies – was not meant to be against them. It was about Rinát. Only about him, for him…

And yes, it left a mark on me that one of my sons previously died in a Hungarian hospital. I gave all my trust and had to pay with my child's life. How could they think that only because so few years had passed, I'd forget it? How could I completely believe them again? How could I once again set foot in the same room where they tried to save him?

I am not a robot; I am a mother. I could say only a mother… but I'm his mother.

And as such, I'm biased regarding what had happened to Nail. Because he is my child, because I must fight for him. And I chose to fight.

Against all attempts to persuade me otherwise, I stood by my decision that Rinát needed to have the best possible chance even if I had to die or give up all I had for that to occur.

We finally ended up in London where a group of doctors in a sarcoma center agreed to treat him. It happened at the Harley Street Hospital, which is a private institution. We had luck. The imaging showed that the disease had not spread. There was no metastasis although the tumor had already grown to almost 20 cm in his left leg.

I was convinced that the immunotherapy was the reason why there were no metastases.

By the time we got to London, Rinát couldn't walk. I rolled him around in a wheelchair, and on the first day, he received morphine compositions eight times a day, besides some muscle relaxants and three types of non-opioid painkillers. He couldn't bend his leg because of the tumor – he had to keep it stretched out. We lived in hotels during the first examinations, and we knew nothing about what was really going to happen to him.

I couldn't speak a word of English, so even hailing a cab proved to be difficult. Not to mention that the first time I had to get around with a wheelchair, I had no knowledge of the area or British culture. When I occasionally left Rinát for an hour to go out for food, I cried all along the way. I was terrified of the future. I was scared for him, and it really bothered me that I couldn't help. Seeing him like this meant such an enormous pain that only those who'd gone through something like this could imagine. I hope nobody ever has to.

A few months ago, Rinát was living a normal teenager's life. He played football, basketball; sports were his everything. Now we were in an alien country, alien environment, in a wheelchair, and we had to rise and rest with eight morphine injections a day and with the promise of an uncertain future. We didn't know whether they would agree to treat him, whether they would operate and whether his leg could be saved. Because back in Hungary a doctor had told me that we shouldn't hesitate to make a decision – we should amputate to give him the best chance of survival. Although he wasn't a child oncologist (he was a doctor in a diagnostics center) but his words had burnt into my heart, my flesh and hadn't left me alone since.

So, our days were spent surviving.

We couldn't have been there without the help of our sponsor. Nor could we have afforded the diagnostics and biopsies. When we left, I had put all former arguments about the foundation aside and told him that I didn't care about anything anymore. He should help me if he could. I begged him to give me a chance to treat Rinát abroad. I had no idea about the costs or the possibilities; I only wanted to flee, flee toward hope, faith, healing… And I thought I could make all those happen in London.

And he agreed to help. Can you believe it? He is a real angel sent by God into my life to help me; otherwise, I would never have met him.

He told me – and I won't forget it as long as I live – "Barbara, I have money. I have a lot of money; you don't have to be afraid. I'll pay for Rinát's treatment, no matter how much it costs."

"But it's possible that it will be so expensive that I will never be able to repay you," I said.

"How much could it cost? $350.000 HUF ($100 million US)? Doesn't matter. I can pay that too…"

Tell me could you hold a grudge against such a man? I fell into his arms and cried, thanking God for bringing this exceptional man into my life. I saw him as a hero, a savior, a messenger of God, a miracle. I didn't care about anything. At that exact moment, he was a miracle for me. A miracle of God, sent by God… he was our guardian angel…

I attracted $100 million US into our life.

Life in London was very challenging for me. I don't speak English. Therefore, I should've hired an interpreter if I've had the money. But I couldn't afford £300 per hour for such services. I carried my laptop with me, and I was constantly searching for open Wi-Fi at the hospital and used Google Translate for communication. I must have been ridiculous, but I had no other choice. I was giving top priority to Rinát's treatment and his recovery. Everything else had become unimportant.

I've never thought that it would be that hard to find an apartment in London. The agencies asked for six or twelve months' deposit, recommendations, and a bank guarantee. The cost of living was unbearably expensive, but I had to find a place for a year where we could stay between the treatments. I talked about these problems with our sponsor, and he was ready to help us. Finally, we managed to rent an apartment near the clinic.

The night before we moved in, I got a call… I'll never ever forget that moment! It was him. Our angel, our mentor, our savior, or hero so far…

He only said one thing: "Get on the next flight and come home," he said. "If you refuse to follow my orders, I won't support the foundation or your son's treatment. If you come home, we can talk about alternative solutions for Rinát's case such as Vienna. There are excellent hospitals there… That's all. Think about it."

I was shocked. A few hours earlier, everything was fine; he even said yes to the apartment. What happened?

I had no idea.

I started crying and begging. Rinát was in a very bad condition, and postponing his treatment would've jeopardized his recovery. I had to give him morphine eight times a day. A new hospital and new diagnoses would've been a massive waste of time. I begged him. I promised him everything, but he was relentless. I felt I was trying to negotiate with a man I'd never known. He was different, and I had no idea what had changed. He mercilessly took advantage of my vulnerability.

Rinát looked at me and said: "We're not going anywhere, right? Don't let me die. Promise me that we'll stay here for my treatment. I know you can make it work."

"We'll stay," I replied, crying. "I'll get the money. I don't know how, but I'll get it. We start your treatment tomorrow morning. Don't worry. Everything will be fine, my darling."

I couldn't sleep that night. My head was full of swirling thoughts. I sent a few more emails, but we couldn't reach an agreement. He even started threatening me. He said that I'd regret it.

"Your London project will fail without me," he added maliciously.

I didn't understand what was happening. I respected this man. We were friends. I was counting on him. I believed that he and his wife would cover our costs in London even though I knew that it would've been an enormous amount, around £25,000 total (approximately $31,188 US). His words were still ringing in my ears:

"Don't worry, Barbara. How much? $100 million US? I have the money. I've told you we'd make it work."

And I believed him, I believed in him. I believed, in the interest of my son's life. In the promise, the nice words, love, his faith. In everything, he meant to me before. "Well," I thought to myself, "so much for angels."

The next day at 5 a.m., we went into the Harley Street Hospital where they started the treatment. I knew that we only had enough money for one, maybe two, days of treatment that should have lasted four days. We had no more money for accommodation; I had no idea where we would rest our head on this Thursday night, me and my cancer patient son in a wheelchair on morphine, in a foreign country, among strangers.

I wrote an email to the Hungarian Embassy – who were within half a mile from us – but didn't receive any meaningful answer. I also looked up a Hungarian celebrity who has a big income from renting flats for Hungarians, but he didn't pick up the phone and didn't answer my text asking for help.

I just sat there while the first few drops of Rinát's chemotherapy drugs dripped down and let myself be swept away in a dreamlike state. I told myself: "God. You know the secrets of my soul…" I hummed a tune from *Stephen, the King*, my favorite rock-opera. "I beg you, show me the way. Send me a sign. I did everything in my power; now I leave our lives in your hands…"

When I came back to reality, a very kind nurse, Lizzy, stepped into our room. She'd been only kind to us ever since we were admitted. I had a sudden idea and turned to her, using my arms and legs and Google Translate to tell her what had happened. That we were left without money, but I didn't want to bring Rinát back home. I asked if there was anyone I could talk to to discuss some kind of repayment options. The next day, Lizzy arranged a meeting between me and the director of finance for the hospital, and I told him the same story. I can't say they were happy, but they told me that there was no way they would kick out a child without treating him – the opposite of what my sponsor said. This was music to my ears. Our sponsor had told me that they would refuse treatment within a few days, and then we'd have to shamefully come back home.

I asked for two months from the director.

That night I sent out about 2000 emails asking for help, all of them written with Google Translate's English. Among the recipients were newspapers, TV stations, Hungarian companies, churches, and private individuals. Anybody in the world I could think of received an email from me. I went to bed that night with the knowledge that I wasn't complete helpless, that I could succeed.

"If God's with me, who's against me?" I repeated my mantra a thousand times over until I finally cried myself to sleep on the hospital bed.

Thursday came, and it was time to leave the hospital, but we had no money or anywhere to sleep. I sat in our room in despair when there was a knock on the door. They told me we had a visitor…

And at that moment, Peter Ellis stepped in, director of the Richard House, a children's hospice located in London. We had met before at a congress in Hungary. He told me that they could give us a place to stay for a few months until we could find something else.

This is how we almost ended up on the streets.

The next day, I talked about my son's disease in public. The TV 2 channel interviewed me, and I was a guest at a radio station. I left all my pride behind.

In June 2013, we celebrated Rinát's twelfth birthday in Pécs. We'd just arrived home from the Harley Street Clinic, London, having paid our bills… I don't even know the total amount of the treatment. For the limb-saving surgery, we would've paid around $68,000 at a different clinic. I kept track of the expenses of chemotherapy until $350,000. I was exhausted, and I wanted the whole procedure to end. During the last block of treatment, Rinát got a CVC infection, in his central venous catheter, and the doctors performed a lifesaving operation on him. It happened on a Saturday afternoon, and they had to call an anesthesiologist from another hospital. We fought against death, and we won. The next day, the nurses hugged me, crying. They thought we'd lose Rinát. When Rinát's parameters got worse, they even had to call the ICU team.

Rinát is a hero. Rinát is a fighter.

I believe that he is still with us only because I chose a well-equipped and well-organized clinic in London instead of a Hungarian hospital. We would've failed otherwise.

It was my best decision to bring him abroad.

I've never seen the $350,000. It was wire transferred directly to the clinic's bank account.

I had been fighting and begging until the Russian Foundation, Rusfond, paid the whole amount – because of Rinát's Russian origins and his Russian dad. I couldn't be more thankful. The money we raised from our Hungarian supporters was used for Rinát's limb-saving surgery and our costs in London.

My faith, my will, my husband's will, our attempts, and prayers made all of these possible.

Our sponsor helped us two more times during the treatment, for which I'm very thankful, but our connection has been lost.

Maybe one day we can sit down together and talk about the reasons…

When it's time…

Angels will be angels…

Rinát is seventeen today. He attends a secondary school in Pécs. He studies English. He has been asymptomatic for five years. He put away his wheelchair and crutch. He took physiotherapy seriously and relearned to walk. At the moment, he goes to crossfit training.

He's just like an average teenager… but not exactly.

Rinát with his coach

He had to grow up too fast. We have to go to hospital for regular controls every four months. He will be fully recovered in 2023. Currently, he is asymptomatic.

They've found a 3.5 cm terime in the right atrium of his heart at the place of the infection, which is very rare, and we should pay attention to it. It is a bit scary, but we've learned to live with fear and put it aside when necessary. He has outgrown his prosthesis, which means that we need to have another limb-saving surgery within a few years either in London, the

USA, or Australia. We are hoping to raise enough money for Rinát's next surgery at the best clinic possible.

Rinát holding his treasured book Think and Grow Rich *by Bob Proctor*

It is also our goal to establish the first real children's hospice in Romonya, Hungary. I'm hoping to raise the necessary funds with the help of my readers worldwide since we're talking about a huge amount, $5,000,000 for the construction and the operating costs of the first two years.

I believe in Nail's immortality. We keep his memory forever. Through the example of Nail's short life and his painful death, Rinát can become a role model for his fellow sufferers, and he can inspire millions of others. Nail's life plan will be completed when Rinát recovers, and the Butterfly Hospice opens its doors.

I'm more than just the chairman of the foundation. Currently, I work as a life coach and motivational trainer. I'm participating in Bob Proctor's coaching and consulting program. I've established Lifechanger Ltd. and am trying to help people to get back on track after failures and to become happy and successful.

Now I know that Nail's death wasn't in vain. I've found peace. I believe that his short life and his death is a lesson for all of us. He has changed our life. He has changed my life. And he has changed the fate of the world.

It is something like the Butterfly Effect that grants the power to cause a hurricane in America to a butterfly flapping its wings in Beijing. Everything and every one of us are interconnected, and our actions can change the world.

Nail is my butterfly...

Barbara Gyura
July 1, 2017

CONTACT INFORMATION

LIFECHANGER LTD.
Give others faith. Lend a helping hand.

Donate now and help annual mentoring of unemployed people and jobseekers, the *Te is lehetsz sikeres*! (You can be successful too!) program.

Bank account no: 12072552-01553574-00100003
For remittance from abroad: IBAN: HU12-12072552-01553574-00100003
Notice: Te is lehetsz sikeres!

www.lifechanger.hu

SUPPORT RINÁT.
Rinát's bank account:
Payee: Haszjanov Rinát
Bank account no: 12072552-01578786-00100007
For remittance from abroad: IBAN: HU37 12072552 01578786 00100007
SWIFT code: UBRT HUHB

READ RINÁT'S BLOG AND SEND HIM A MESSAGE:
www.helprinat.hu

GRAB A STARTER PACK!
Place your donation box in your workplace or local shop and help raise money.

Buy our thank-you sweets, and support the construction of the Butterfly House.

If you wish to donate directly to Light of My Eyes Foundation, our banking details are as follows:

Name of the foundation: Light of My Eyes Foundation
Postal address: Gém u. 7. – 7634 – Pécs – Hungary
Account handling bank: Szigetvári Takarékszövetkezet
Bank account no: 50800111 11083762
For remittance from abroad: IBAN: HU24 50800111 11083762 00000000
– SWIFT code: TAKBHUHB

Bank address: Bajcsy-Zsilinszky E. utca 7. – 7622 – Pécs / Hungary
Account handling bank: UniCredit Bank
Bank account no: 10918001 00000033 67470006
For remittance from abroad: IBAN: HU77 10918001 00000033 67470006
– SWIFT code: BACXHUHB
Bank address: Szabadság tér 5-6. – 1054 – Budapest / Hungary

Your donations will be spent supporting families who have been touched by life-threatening or life-shortening conditions. Every dollar counts in our efforts to reduce the burden of disease. You can support our charity by PayPal as well.

MORE INFORMATION
Szemem Fénye Alapítvány (Light of My Eyes Foundation)
Address: H-7634 Pécs, Rácvárosi út 37.
Email: vallalati@szemefenye.hu
Tel: +36-72/526-658

CHARITY SHOP
You can donate children's and adult clothes, toys, and household devices to support our mission.

Please send your donation to the following address:
H-7634 Pécs, Rácvárosi út 37.
Tel.: +36-72/251-532
Email: charityshop@szemefenye.hu
Web: www.szememfenye.hu

LET'S BUILD A CHILDREN'S HOSPICE TOGETHER.
The children's hospice complex will cost an approximate net amount of $5 million US.

Please, if you can, support the realization of the Butterfly Children's Hospice House with money!

Szemem Fénye Alapítvány (Light of My Eyes Foundation)
Bank account no: 50800111 11083762
For remittance from abroad: IBAN: HU24-50800111-11083762-00000000
SWIFT code: TAKB HUHB

Tax 1%: 18321407-2-02

Web: www.newhospice.hu
www.szememfenye.hu

For further information, you can find me at **www.gyurabarbara.com** and **www.lifechanger.hu**. You can also visit our website at **www.szememfenye.hu** or find us on Facebook at **www.facebook.com/szememfenyealapitvany**. If you would like to contact me directly, please email **gyurabarbara@szememfenye.hu**.

There are children who are not given a long life.
We are for them and for those who love them the most.

ABOUT THE AUTHOR

Barbara Gyura, Hungary's first facilitator of the world-famous, American Thinking Into Results Program, has been helping people create the life they want to live and fulfill their most secret dreams.

Barbara works very enthusiastically with individuals, with groups, also with companies and enterprises to guide her clients in discovering their deepest desires and goals, their hidden potentials, and being able to achieve their personal and business goals.

She has been studying the psychology of personal growth and development for more than 30 years, and she has worked together with more than 500 people in the past 22 years. As an entrepreneur and as a foundation leader she has directed 50-70 employees and has established Hungary's pediatric patients' transportation and the children's hospice movement. She has built and runs Hungary's first Children's Hospice House (www.szememfenye.hu).

She is passionate about bringing people to the maximum. Her strong character, charismatic personality guarantees the maximum support for her clients, so that they can live healthy, energetic lives full of abundance and happiness.

Barbara has nearly two-decades' experience in the field of for- and non-profit business, where her main areas of professional interest are the leadership attitude and skills, planning and organizing, deputation, communication, the balance of work and private life and time management. She has been supporting her clients as a life – and business coach for years, and in the last year she has become the official representative and consultant of the worldwide most successful life success company, The Proctor Gallagher Institute.

She is a bestseller writer. The book, which has the title, *Light of my Eyes: Nail*, is being published this year on the American book market.

At present she is also dealing with the coaching of teenagers, Hungarian and foreign students', who participate in tertiary education, educational coaching, children's coaching, partner relationship coaching and also VIP (famous people) coaching.

Barbara is an intensely growth – and goal – oriented professional, has a solution-oriented way of thinking, who is passionate about supporting people on their way towards their dreams. She is a strict and consistent coach, who does not know impossible.

If you would like to create the life you've been dreaming of, either as a private person, or as a company co-worker or leader, contact her by email address at gyurabarbara@lifechanger.hu .

www.ingramcontent.com/pod-product-compliance
Lightning Source LLC
LaVergne TN
LVHW051118080426
835510LV00018B/2099